BRUCE

SPRINGSTEEN

BRUCE SPRINGSTEEN

Marianne Meyer

A **2M** Communications
Production

BALLANTINE BOOKS ● NEW YORK

Library of Congress Catalog Card Number: 84-90987

ISBN 0-345-32218-5

Manufactured in the United States of America

First Ballantine Books Edition: October 1984

Front cover photo by Ross Marino
Back cover photo © 1981 by Lynn Goldsmith/LGI Inc.
Interior book design by Michaelis/Carpelis Design

FOR TERRY, with all the madness in my soul

CONTENTS

ACKNOWLEDGMENTS

The material in this book was gathered from first-hand interviews, from interviews and notes shared with me by fellow writers and fans, and from written and broadcast accounts of Bruce Springsteen's career. My sincere thanks to all the generous people and publications who gave me additional insight, information, and enthusiasm for this project.

A few specifics: Jeff Tamarkin, editor, friend, and more. (I may still forgive you, J.T.); John Hammond, a man whose manners are like his musical taste—impeccable; Jimmy B, for letting me out from "Under the Lights" and for his invaluable rolodex; Gina and Mary Beth, "atmosphere soakers" extraordinaire; Ken Viola (I still owe ya lunch) and Lou Cohan, for a fanzine equal to the name Thunder Road; Mike Greenblatt, for my "start" (?!) in show-biz, and the inside story; Brian Chin, for good conversation and great insight; "Those

Who Have" (and a few who haven't)—Schiffy, Shari, Katie, Genie, Andys P&B, Tricia, Mary, Julie, Eileen, Sue, Stephen, Sharon, Lenny, Glenn, and the gang; Lois, for her "keyboard" contribution (Kathryn, too); Gary DaSilva, for being a good guy as well as a legal eagle; JVZ and Jerry, who may never know; Howard B. Leibowitz, who will.

A few who stand apart:

Special thanks and much love to my family—Kay, who knows more about Bruce than any mother except his own should have to; Henry, who'll say "that's nice"; Thom, Kathy, Muriel, et al (Poltracks, too!) for their contagious warmth and pride. And to Tootie, who smiles on us all.

Bruce Springsteen is a rare performer who reaches out to those he's never met and makes them feel he'd be glad for the opportunity. To him, my respect, admiration, thanks (and maybe just a little lust...) for making wonderful, magical music and for inspiring more positive emotions than these pages could express.

Lastly, but everlasting, my best to the man who brings it out in me. Terry, no thanks are enough for your tenderness and loving care. Will all my love do?

MY HOMETOWN

Visit Paris, and you can pick up postcards of the Eiffel Tower. Go to London, and you can stock up on glossies of Big Ben and Buckingham Palace. But if you're hanging out on the boardwalk in Asbury Park, New Jersey, it's the Bruce Springsteen postcards that will grab your attention.

Check it out—sitting in the wire rack of one of those tacky shops that sell everything from rubber snakes to salt and pepper shakers in the shape of private female anatomy, there's one postcard in particular that sells really well these days. On a field of neon orange and blue, the carnival letters read: "Greetings from Asbury Park, N.J.," the same cheery legend, the same fading-summer spirit that adorned the cover of Bruce's first album. But now, when you turn it over, you don't read about Asbury Park's one-time position as a high-class amusement park playland and summer home by the

sea. Now you read that "Asbury Park is Bruce Springsteen's home town."

Asbury Park, zip code 07712, a once-budding resort
town plying the tourist trade with hotels, beaches, fun
houses, and the promise of summertime romance.
Nowadays, it's little more than New Jersey's version
of Coney Island, fifty miles from Manhattan, the kind
of place tourists remark upon sadly as they pass through.
Asbury Park still smarts from the headlines it made in
the early '70s, when race riots ravaged its reputation.
Visiting here, you understand more fully the final track
on *Born in the U.S.A.*, Bruce's bittersweet reminis-
cence for "My Hometown."

Actually, nearby Freehold, N.J., holds the honor of
being Bruce's birthplace, but the presence of Springsteen in Asbury Park is too strong for Freehold to fight
back. Asbury Park is where Bruce hung out for the
better part of his teenage years, hustling gigs in the
boardwalk bars with his first rock and roll bands. And
today, in those same bars, the talk still revolves around
that local boy and his music. In the Stone Pony, a
comfy bar located right behind the site of the old roller
coaster on the boardwalk, it's almost a religion. The
music of Bruce, Southside Johnny, Gary U.S. Bonds,
Little Steven Van Zandt, and Clarence Clemons and
the Red Bank Rockers has virtually no competition on
the booming sound system. Walk back past three of
the four brick bars and there's a little spot with a photo
collage of "The Boss" and his buddies. As one weekend
pilgrim to the spot put it, "All they need is a kneeling
pad and they've got themselves a shrine."

But who can blame them? New Jersey, long the butt
of nasty jokes and New York sneers—comedian Robert
Klein once called it "ten miles of cosmic fart on the

other side of the river"—has finally got itself a post-Sinatra hero of the first order. John Scher, New Jersey-based concert promoter who's handled many of the Garden State Springsteen concerts of the last ten years, gives Bruce a lot of the credit for turning that attitude around. "There was a time in the late sixties and early seventies when you felt a lot of chauvinism about being from Jersey," he said in 1981. "After the popularity Bruce obtained, you weren't afraid to say 'Yeah, I'm from Jersey.' He was one of the first people for the kids to identify with, to be proud of."

But the fans who pour into Asbury Park to soak up the vicarious Springsteen vibes come from all over, not just Jersey. Bruce has become a bona fide superstar throughout the world; even the Swedish fans know about Madame Marie, (of "4th of July/Sandy" fame) the gypsy fortune teller who still plies her hand-reading wares on the arcade strip. And unlike most "home town legends" who split for greener pastures when their muse helps them make it, Bruce still lives in the South Jersey region and might walk by Madame Marie's any moment now. For a platinum-selling star, he still has simple tastes, a fondness for greasy burgers and fat-fried chicken and a love of crisp open-air days on the beach. He might just be out there, treading the creaky wooden boardwalk, but if you see him, you'll be amazed at his quiet, shy demeanor. Ask him what he's doing here, cruising along the ocean, and he'll probably just smile. "I live here. What's your excuse?"

That's one of the most remarkable things about Springsteen. On record, he's one of the most lyrical, intelligent, musically powerful singer/songwriter/guitarists that the rock era has produced. On stage, he burns up the boards with an intensity, joy, and sheer animal exhuberance that is unparalleled in today's concert scene. But take him out of the performer's context, and he's, well . . . a nice guy.

A nice guy who also happens to have seven gold and/or platinum albums to his credit, and a fanatical following that makes his worldwide concert tours into full-fledged media events. That he can balance the two in a music scene where ego-tripping is par for the course is part of the man's mystique. Fred Schruers, a *Rolling Stone* reporter who met Bruce in 1981, said, "There is finally something irrevocably lonely and restless about him." E Street Band pianist Roy Bittan described him thus: "He's so unlike everything you think a real successful rock star would be."

He's not much of a drinker—a couple of beers and he's talking loose and silly. He doesn't smoke and has spoken out against drugs of any kind. He's gone out with a number of attractive, talented women, but usually with a discreet, nearly courtly manner that makes for dull gossip-column chatter. After a wildly exhausting show, he'll stand patiently signing autographs and answering questions for the fans waiting outside the arena, and he is more likely to head out on a midnight burger run than to get caught up in wild backstage debauchery.

If he were the type to do endorsements (he's not), one of the fast-food chains would probably be a natural. "I never did get comfortable with places that got the menu in the window," he has said, and he can knock down quarter-pounders in record time.

For excitement, he's into roller coasters and softball games (he's a good player), pool, pinball games, and fast cars. He likes the club scene, but for the music, not the celebrity chit-chat. Socking down the Pepsis, he'll check out a variety of performers, from the Clash and U2 to local acts like Beaver Brown who play the Pony regularly.

The Stone Pony, in fact, is one of Bruce's favorite places to hang out. It's not a long drive from his new house, the boardwalk is right across the street, and, best of all, nobody there will make a big deal of it if he wants to sit and relax and hear some live music.

"In the summer, it's a little different, because there's a lot of tourists, kids, who aren't used to seeing him on a regular basis," said one Pony regular. "They'll ask him for an autograph, and he'll talk to whoever talks to him. But usually, he walks in the door and nobody reacts. Sometimes he'll even go behind the bar and bartend."

There are special nights, too, when Bruce gets up and jams with the local acts he really enjoys, groups like Diamonds or Cats on a Smooth Surface.

Gina Esposito, who grew up in New Jersey and knows Asbury Park as only the natives do, recalls one particular night when Bruce rocked the Stone Pony. One might even say he did it at her request:

"It was a Sunday night, in July of 1983, and Bruce was just sitting by the bar by himself and listening to Cats. The band even did the Mitch Ryder medley and I thought for sure he was going to get up and play, but he wasn't moving. There was nobody on either side of him, the barstools were empty all night, and he was just nursing his drink. I almost felt sorry for him—it was like he had nobody to talk to—but maybe he was happy like that, that nobody bothered him.

"Anyway, I guess he just wasn't in the mood to play; it was already three o'clock, and time to start getting people out of there. Bruce was right in front of us walking out the door, and so we're all walking out and down the street that runs alongside the Stone Pony, and the stage door is right there." Gina pauses to laugh. "I don't know what possessed me, but he was right there at arm's length, and I tapped him on the shoulder and said, 'Ah, Bruce, you shoulda *played*.'

"Some of the guys in the band were standing near the stage door, and Bruce just turned around, walked right over to them, and said, 'You guys wanna play one more?'

"So he walks in, the place is now three-quarters empty, and we duck in right behind him. And he played for about a half-hour—a ten-minute version of 'Twist and Shout,' a couple of oldies—he was incredible. When he'd been sitting at the bar, he was so quiet, but when he got up there, he just went nuts, smiling and laughing... Then, when he finished playing, he took the guitar off and he just *ran* out the stage door and into the bar just down the street. We figured he was just staying there until the crowd died down."

Gina shakes her head. "I still don't believe it. Bruce Springsteen, just *playing*, in a small club like that." When he does, it's almost always great oldies and favorite cover tunes.

His own music takes its spirit from a variety of sources, many of them much deeper and more complex than his pop culture sounds and "common-folk" lyrical narratives would suggest. "I'm nuts about the movies," Bruce admitted, but when he talks about John Ford westerns or the film versions of John Steinbeck's novels, he's not talking about crunching popcorn in the balcony. He admires the story-telling ability of the authors and directors, the style with which they reveal the drama of everyday life, and he works toward similar ends in his songs. Just like the movies, those glittering shadow images that convey powerful messages in the guise of escapist entertainment, Bruce Springsteen's songs are more than just AM/FM radio fodder.

Sure, his upbeat anthems are the perfect soundtrack to a summer night spent driving, radio on, but then his ballads smolder with the realization that all the running is exhausting and, but for love, often futile. While many rock stars delight in singing about life in the fast lane, Bruce knows what it feels like to be stalled in the stop-and-go details of daily living, and he has succeeded in reaching an extraordinary audience for his efforts. To younger fans who want the pure adrenaline rush of buzz-saw guitar and arena rock hysteria, he's a hero. But he's also a champion for the older, more settled crowd, who value his empathy with their problems.

When those forces get together—Bruce and his fans—the result is sheer rock and roll magic. Describing it is nearly impossible; a Bruce fan will quickly divide the world into "Those Who've Seen Him" and "Those Who Haven't." In the former group, supporters turn critique into hyperbole, and even those who grudgingly attend a show are bound to convert to some degree of admiration.

For "Those Who Haven't," perhaps the easiest way to appreciate the special qualities of a Springsteen concert is to consider him in relation to most other concert headliners. For a start, he doesn't headline in the usual sense of putting on a prepackaged ninety-minute set that relies on a support act to give the fans their money's worth. Bruce and the E Street Band will play for nearly four hours, with a half-hour intermission, and will carry the crowd through that time period without any special effects, laser gimmickry, or elaborate set changes. Beyond simple yet stunning lighting design, all of the drama and excitement is generated by the music and enthusiasm of the band itself, in conjunction with the audience.

The audience is as much a part of Springsteen's shows as he is. The energy flows in an alternating current between the stage and the stands, with Bruce as the fuse and each member of the crowd a part of the conduit. And when "The Boss" and Clarence take off on one of their joking jags, everyone can join in the laughter. Sometimes it's a spontaneous slide, Bruce taking off from a speaker and landing right at the "Big Man's" feet, and then it's like a new discovery of rock's carefree joys. Sometimes they get into a piece of shtick that's been performed so often, it's the physical equivalent of a song—the hand-clapping a cappella break of "Rosalita" or the Romeo and Juliet tease of "Fire." Sure, they're repetitions, but three chords have always been the backbone of rock, and Bruce is nothing if not true to rock tradition.

You can hear it in the cover tunes he plays when the whim hits him, everything from Buddy Holly to Creedence Clearwater Revival to the Rolling Stones and back again to the Dovells ("You Can't Sit Down"). He loves that sweet rock and soul of any era (but particularly the '50s and '60s), and you can hear elements of it in the roller-rink organ of "Ramrod," the frat-rock rowdiness of "Sherry Darling," or his classic Mitch Ryder medley. But you can also hear a contemporary American Gothic vision in "Racing in the Streets" or "Born in the U.S.A."

Whether you come to a Springsteen show for the ballads or the rockers, or merely out of curiosity, you won't go away empty-handed. Every time Springsteen plays it's like a party with the record collection of your dreams, and anyone who likes their rock and roll played with heart and soul is invited.

During his 1984 concert tour, in support of the *Born in the U.S.A.* album, 202,000 people were invited to Bruce Springsteen's homecoming party. In an unprecedented ten-night stand at New Jersey's Byrne Meadowlands Arena, Bruce played before his hometown on the grandest scale ever and still was able to connect with his crowd as if they were that tiny batch of late-night stragglers in the Stone Pony.

Each evening, when twenty thousand voices shouted out the unofficial New Jersey state anthem, "Born to Run," you could feel the chill of local pride in the August night. It was Bruce Springsteen's hometown triumph, pure and simple, and it was made even sweeter by the fact that it wasn't always this way. In fact, when Bruce Springsteen had been a young boy growing up, not fifty miles away from this sold-out concert hall, it seemed as if success would never come to pass. . . .

GROWIN' UP

*O*n September 23, 1949, Adele and Douglas Springsteen celebrated the arrival of their firstborn child, and only son. They named him Bruce. In years to come, he would be followed by two sisters—Ginny (one year later) and Pam (thirteen years younger)—and a cloud of trouble that caused his parents a great deal of concern.

He wasn't a wild child or a mean-spirited one, but more of an independent kid, thinking for himself and asking the kind of questions that didn't sit well in the parochial grammar schools of a little town like Freehold, New Jersey.

"In the third grade, a nun stuffed me into a garbage can she kept under her desk because she told me that's where I belonged," Bruce once told *Newsweek* magazine. "I also had the distinction of being the only altar boy knocked down by a priest on the steps of the altar during Mass. The old priest got mad. My mom wanted me to learn how to serve Mass, but I didn't know what I was doin' so I was tryin' to fake it." Schooling never came easy to young Bruce.

"I hated school. I had the big hate," he said simply. The same unhappy scenes would repeat themselves— after school, the nuns would take Bruce to the convent and send Ginny home to fetch their parents. Mrs. Springsteen would come and get Bruce; Mr. Springsteen would wait at home and glare at his troublemaker son. When he was about eleven, Bruce started running away from home, but his parents would find him every time and bring him home again, to the little house on Institute Street.

It was a place that needed a paint job and smelled of a nearby Nestle's factory. "Man, when it rained, we smelled that stuff all day long," he told *The Aquarian*'s Mike Greenblatt in a home-town tour/interview. Driving through the string of small towns that are scattered throughout South Jersey, he admitted to being relatively rootless in his youngest days. "Yeah, I lived in practically every single town around here, from Atlantic Highland to Bradley Beach. We used to move quite often."

The Springsteens were relatively poor and frequently moved in with Bruce's grandparents while they struggled to make ends meet. Financially, they never had it easy—Douglas Springsteen (the name is Dutch, but his family is mostly Irish) was a tough man who worked many jobs in an attempt to support his family, but they never came easy or for long. He worked in a factory and as a gardener and a prison guard.

Adele (whose background was Italian), on the other hand, had the same secretarial job since she left high school at age eighteen, and she would continue to work at it all through Bruce's childhood. When Bruce speaks of his mother in interviews, he does it with solid respect. "She's real tough," he said once, "but she never lost her sweetness. It's kinda amazing." Sometimes he even looks embarrassed. "Look, I mean you could call it corny or somethin', but a woman like my mother is a real inspiration to me."

It was Mom who gave Bruce his first sweet blast of rock and roll. Adele Springsteen was only in her late twenties when Bruce was a child, and, as he described it, "She was an Elvis Presley fan. She used to listen to him on the radio. Every morning in my house, you'd come down before you'd go to school, my mother's cookin' up the breakfast, got the radio on, on top of the refrigerator, tuned to the AM station."

The sounds on the radio captivated Bruce—the way Roy Orbison sang could break your heart with its lonesome beauty; there was the magnificent "sensurround" sound of producer Phil Spector's work for the Crystals and the Ronettes; and that wild, thumping drum that Bo Diddley used in his records. But no one could match Elvis, the King.

"See, I was nine years old when I saw Elvis on 'Ed Sullivan,'" Bruce explained, "and I had to get a guitar the *next day*. I stood in front of my mirror with that guitar on...and I knew then that's what had been missing." Bruce wanted to be like his hero—"Anybody who sees Elvis Presley and doesn't want to be like Elvis Presley has to have something wrong with him," Bruce insisted—but as a nine-year-old he couldn't do it. His fingers were too small to make the chords he wanted to play, and he put the guitar down, discouraged. "But then it was like I crawled back into the grave until I was thirteen. Someone once did an article interviewing my classmates and they all said I seemed a million miles away. I had very few friends. I mostly kept to myself."

Bruce was a loner, the kind of kid who didn't feel he fit in with any of the cliques around him. "There were groups like the rah-rahs and the greasers," he remembered, "and I bounced back and forth, trying to figure out where I fit in. I didn't dig the scene that either had happening. So consequently, I didn't do anything; I just kinda was."

"I was funny," he told SOUNDS magazine. "I was the kind of kid that never got into trouble, but trouble would gravitate around me—not even serious stuff, only ridiculous kinds of things. I didn't have anything to hold on to, or any connections whatsoever—I was just reeling through space and bouncing off the walls and bouncing off people—until rock and roll and the guitar. And when I found that, it was like I was home free, and the other stuff just didn't matter anymore."

It happened when Bruce was thirteen and the radio on top of the refrigerator started giving forth new sounds, imported from England and bearing the exotic names of groups like the Beatles, the Rolling Stones, and the Animals. "That really kicked it off for me," he said. Bruce got another guitar, and this time he *could* make his fingers duplicate the magic sounds. He was hooked, and wouldn't leave the guitar again. "I used to love to just open the case because of the way it smelled," he recalled fondly. "Oh man, in the middle of the house, and furniture polish and cabbage and all, it smelled like somethin' new, and it was a mysterious THING."

Bruce saw his parents struggling; he saw small-town compromises and frustrations; he felt the resentment of his classmates and teachers directed at him because he thought differently than they did—but that guitar seemed to change it all. "I found something that was like a key to a little door that said, 'There's more to it than this. There's more to it than just living that way.'"

It didn't thrill Bruce's parents, however, that he wanted to be a rocker. "When I was a boy," he often stops in the middle of concert performances of "Growin' Up" to say, "there were two things in my house that my parents didn't like. One was me. The other was the guitar. 'That goddam guitar!' my father used to say. I think he thought all the things in my room were made by the same company—'that goddam guitar, the goddam stereo, those goddam records. . . .'" There is still a bit of the Catholic boy in Bruce, and he'll tell of going to meet God, on the advice of the Catholic priest, to try to sort out the confusion with his parents. "God, ya gotta help me," he'll say. "My mother wants me to be a lawyer . . . and all I wanna do is play my guitar." In concert, God answers Bruce in a way that he could have only dreamed of when he was a confused young boy. . . . "All of a sudden," Bruce goes on, "there's this light in the sky above me, and a great big voice booms out and says"—the music stops—"LET IT ROCK!" Jumping back into the song, Bruce brings all the audience with him as he celebrates the freedom and joyful power of rock and roll.

It wasn't always funny, though. Some of Bruce's other songs and concerts fairly mythologize the tensions that are common between ambitious young men and their equally determined fathers. "He used to come down on me real hard," Bruce admitted once, and he built a fierce, deeply affecting concert rap around the fights they'd have in the early morning/late night when teenager Bruce would try to slip in the house unnoticed:

"... I would slick my hair back real tight so he couldn't tell how long it was gettin' and try to sneak through the kitchen. But the old man would catch me every night and he'd drag me back into the kitchen and make me sit down at that table in the dark.... I always remember sitting there and I could always hear his voice but I could never, ever see his face. We'd start off talking about nothing much, how I was doin' but pretty soon he'd ask me what I thought I was doin', with myself and we'd always end up screaming at each other and my mother, she'd always end up runnin' in from the front room crying tryin' to stop us from fightin' with each other. And I'd always end up runnin' out the back door screamin', tellin' him, tellin' him, tellin' him that it was my life and I was gonna do what I wanted to do...."

While the tone of these childhood stories veer from the comic to the bitter, Bruce stressed that both are accurate. "It's just a different side of the same experience. Having a little distance, I still feel both ways about those experiences. I sort of have a perspective on those times right now, maybe a little more than I did then."

For all the hard times, Bruce's parents always stayed together and made a home for the three kids. And for all the rebellion and arguments, Bruce never forgot that. "My mother and father," he told Fred Schruers, "they've got a very deep love because they know and understand each other in a very realistic way."

Ultimately, Bruce and his father reached a similar understanding, and Bruce frequently speaks of his dad in concert. "It took thirty years for us to say we loved each other," he told an audience in 1981. "If you've got parents at home, ask them what they're thinking. You might be surprised."

In his own teen years, Bruce probably would have found it hard to follow that advice.

"By the end of high school," he told *Crawdaddy* magazine, "I didn't have much to do with anybody. I almost didn't graduate because the kids in my class wouldn't let me. I was playing in bands and my hair was real long, and the sister got up in front of everybody and said, 'Class, don't you have any pride in yourselves? Are you going to allow this boy to embarrass you and go to graduation looking like that?' And they weren't gonna let me graduate unless I cut my hair. So, on the day of graduation I left the house and I didn't come back." (He'd forgotten, though, about a family graduation party; his mom tracked him down at a friend's house in New York City and dragged him home for another awkward evening.)

The scene fairly repeated itself in college. Bruce was enrolled for one semester at Ocean County Community College, about twenty miles south of Freehold. Near the end of his first term, he was called into the guidance counselor's office. The man wanted to know what the trouble was. "Things are great, I feel fine," Bruce told him.

"Then why do you look like that?" the counselor asked, pointing to Bruce's standard attire—plain white undershirt, tight jeans, sneakers, and leather jacket. "There are some students who have . . . complained about you."

"Well, that's their problem, ya know?" Bruce said in reply, but the damage had been done. That would be his first—and last—attempt at the college life.

If he looked like a rebel, though, Bruce Springsteen had one thing the James Dean–type heroes didn't have—a cause. He decided to follow "the only thing that was ever true, the only thing that never let me down—rock and roll." That would be his career. After all, he had experience. He had been in his first money-making band when he was just sixteen.

I'M A ROCKER

*M*arion Vinyard thought that the noise might drive her crazy. Her home, in one half of a three-story duplex of Freehold, was reverberating with a booming sound that came from the other half. It was a group of kids with guitars, drums, and other instruments of musical torture, and they were trying—rather unsuccessfully—to play rock and roll. Finally, she asked her husband, Tex, to go next door and tell them to knock it off.

A tough-talking guy with a soft heart, Tex came back to tell her what a nice group of kids they were. Marion saw for herself when the rhythm guitarist, George Theiss, stopped by a few days later to apologize, and suddenly the rehearsals were taking place in the Vinyard living room, with Tex acting as manager for the band. They called themselves the Castiles, after the soap George used in his hair, and it soon became clear that they needed a new guitarist to fill out their developing sound.

Word got around, and then, one rainy night, a skinny kid named Bruce Springsteen knocked on the Vinyard door and volunteered his services. His long dark hair drooping down over bad adolescent skin, Bruce shyly told Tex that he knew a few chords and a little lead guitar, but he hastened to add that he was "quick to learn." He ran through a few songs with George and Frank, the Castiles' bass player, and asked anxiously if he could be in the band.

Tex liked the kid—they shared a love of Elvis and drive-in movies—but he told Bruce he should come back after he'd learned five songs. Bruce was back the next night and blew them away with nearly a dozen. He repeated the feat a few days later for the rest of the group, too shy even to notice how the drummer had dropped his sticks in amazement when Bruce began to play. Yeah, they said eagerly when Bruce asked again. You can be in the band.

About a month and a half later, the new Castiles had their first gig, at a swim club, and they took home the grand amount of thirty-five dollars for their efforts. The boys insisted on giving Tex three fifty. After all, ten percent was the going rate for managers at the time. Obviously not in the game for money, Tex continued to look after the Castiles, getting them local talent shows, gigs performing before the feature at the Loew's drive-in movie, and the occasional midnight show at the local Shop Rite supermarket.

The Castiles even cut a single—"That's What You Get" backed with "Baby I," two tunes that Bruce and George wrote in the back seat of a car on the way to Bricktown Mall shopping center, where they would be recording. The single was never released, though—a deal for a recording contract fell through when Tex and the boys got suspicious about having to put up front money themselves.

Still, for a bunch of teenagers, they did well. The Castiles became quite popular on the local club circuit and even got a plum booking in New York City, where Lovin' Spoonful leader John Sebastian and some guys from the Young Rascals came to see them. The fun faded when high school ended, and the Castiles broke up in 1967. Bruce never forgot Tex and Marion, though. When the rest of the Springsteen family took off for California—Douglas was heading for a new job as a bus driver in San Mateo—Bruce stayed behind and was a frequent visitor to the Vinyard household. He told his surrogate parents all about the new bands he was involved with.

The first was Earth, a power rock band inspired by the tough new sounds of bands like Cream and the electrifying guitar of Jimi Hendrix. While playing with Earth, Bruce frequently ran across another new band, Moment of Truth, a Sgt. Peppers'-type band, which included drummer Vini Lopez and rhythm guitarist Garry Tallent. Lopez's previous band, Sonny Kenn and the Starfires, had once beaten the Castiles (the Starfires took second place, the Castiles third) in a battle of the bands at the Keyport Rollerdome, and the friendly rivalry grew to a working friendship among the young musicians. There was a genuine scene developing along the Jersey shore, with numerous bands playing in the beach bars. The constantly shifting personnel brought new blood, and new sounds with them.

One of the best places to hang out was The Upstage Club, located on Cookman Avenue in Asbury Park. A guy named Tom Potter had opened the place in 1968, and it quickly became a mecca for local musicians. It was really two clubs in one—the downstairs coffee house had food, soft drinks, and mostly acoustic music, but the upstairs was where the action was. Climbing the narrow staircase lined with day-glo posters, you could smell smoke and hear a rocking jam session going on almost any night of the week. "Southside Johnny" Lyon, one of the regulars, called it "a petri dish for the bacteria of rock and roll."

Recalling the scene for *Rolling Stone*'s John Milward, Southside said: "Groups would form and break up at the drop of a hat and, in a way, Asbury's Upstage Club symbolized these quick musical changes. For a few years in the late sixties when the bars closed at two A.M., everybody would rush to the Upstage from their other gigs for some serious jamming. We'd assemble a band and put together a set, with some nights coming out real hot and others blowing cold."

Anyone who wanted to could get up on stage and play, but, like a scene from an old western movie, each new guitarslinger was eyed suspiciously until he proved himself. It didn't take long for Bruce to establish himself as the fastest draw in town. "I first heard him in 1968," Southside remembered. "I thought he really had it. He was one of the most natural rock 'n' roll giants I've ever seen. He had charisma. I don't think you'll meet anybody in Asbury Park who didn't believe he was going all the way."

Garry Tallent would second that emotion. "We always thought Bruce was a good act. If there was a chance of any of us making a living through music, we figured it would have to happen through him."

Earth was a short-lived band, but Bruce carried on

the heavy rock sound with his next band, Child, formed
in 1969. Lopez, who had disbanded Moment of Truth,
came aboard on drums; Danny Federici, an organ player
from Passaic, N.J., joined, too, along with a bass player
named Vini Roslyn. When it was discovered that a
Long Island band had first claim to the name Child,
the guys got together and tossed around ideas for the
band's new moniker. Bruce, the unofficial leader,
thought Steel Mill sounded good, and so that's what
they became.

Kids on the Jersey shore still talk about Steel Mill
with reverence, and its regional success in the area at
the time was quite extraordinary for an unsigned band.
With Bruce's blues-oriented guitar at the forefront, Steel
Mill was an early amalgam of heavy metal, country
twang, Chuck Berry rockers, and muscular jamming,
like the illegitimate child of some musical orgy among
Lynyrd Skynyrd, Allman Brothers, and Humble Pie.

Steve Van Zandt (who'll enter this tale very soon)
remembers Steel Mill as being "one of the very first
heavy metal bands before heavy metal really happened, so it had the very, very early elements of it.
We had a bit more melody and a bit more to the lyrical
side of it than a lot of the hardcore stuff today." (His-
torians take note: There was a song called "Garden
State Parkway Blues" in the Steel Mill repertoire—
even then, Bruce's songwriting efforts paid homage to
his home state.)

The look of the band would cause current Springsteen fans to gasp in wonder. It was strictly country
hippie—Bruce in faded, patched denims, and clean-
shaven, but with a long, shaggy mane of wavy hair that
fell well below his shoulders. If the band had the look
of wacked-out flower children, Bruce himself made it

clear that he would have none of the nonmusical trappings of psychedelia. Then, as now, he was firmly against the use of drugs of any kind. The music was the only high he needed.

Other people were getting off on it as well. Steel Mill became a hot ticket playing to jammed houses at the Upstage, Student Prince, Sunshine Inn, and even some of the community colleges in Monmouth and Ocean counties. When they opened for Grand Funk Railroad, they held their own admirably. One local music critic, Joan Pikula of the *Asbury Park Press*, concluded, "There are going to be lots of rock groups in the area come this summer—some of the best. If you have to make a choice between the best of them and Steel Mill, you'd end up ahead of the game if you choose this group."

Encouraged by the good words—and by Bruce, who wanted to visit his parents—Steel Mill headed west to try their luck in California. "We traveled in this old Chevy truck," Bruce recalled, "with all the equipment in the back and about one hundred bucks each, and as a matter of fact, we played the Filmore on audition night. We played two Tuesdays, and we opened up the show. Nils Lofgren played one night; he was auditioning, too. He was great." Nearly fourteen years later, they'd share the same stage—and a whole new set of circumstances—when Nils would join the E Street Band for a world concert tour. But in those days, both guitarists were struggling for attention.

Steel Mill made small progress in their California quest. The Matrix offered them a semiregular gig opening for people like Boz Scaggs and Elvin Bishop. Bill Graham liked the Filmore performance enough to offer the group a studio audition, and he made tapes of some original Steel Mill songs: "He's Guilty," "Train Ride," "Goin' Back to Georgia." He was even interested in signing the group to an official recording contract. The band, however, thought the advance money was too little, too late. They returned to New Jersey on borrowed money, clutching a favorable review from *San Franciso Examiner* critic Phillip Elwood—"I have never been so overwhelmed by totally unknown talent"—which promptly went into the windows of hometown clubs.

"It was a big deal, it was a big adventure," Bruce laughed when it was all over. "We came back to New Jersey and it was like, 'Hey, we been to California!' As a matter of fact, we used to advertise that on the shows when we came back—'Back from California!' That was the thing in those days, if you went out and you came back and you had a review." To the laid-back beach crowd at the boardwalk, it *was* a rather impressive accomplishment. "I didn't know anybody who *ever* made a record.... Nobody had ever done anything too much, and so it was like a whole 'nother world, ya know?" Bruce told one interviewer. "I don't think I ever knew anybody who ever, like, went to Pennsylvania!"

Actually, Richmond, Virginia, was becoming a home away from home for the Asbury Park bands, providing another strip of bars that offered jobs to young musicians. Robbin Thompson, a Virginian from a band called Mercy Flight, joined Steel Mill as a lead vocalist when they returned from California, and there was talk of the band relocating permanently to the Richmond area, but they never made the southern switch.

Vince Roslyn left the band to be replaced by a talented local guy named Steve Van Zandt. Van Zandt had started his musical career on rhythm guitar and had experience as a lead singer, guitar player, piano player, and more. Though Steel Mill required his services on bass, Van Zandt's multi-instrumental abilities would come to play a large role in Bruce Springsteen's future—and in a tight friendship between the two young men.

When Asbury Park was badly burned in race riots in the summer of 1970, Steel Mill's spark seemed to fizzle, much like the city's tourist trade. The band officially broke up in early 1971, and Bruce got involved in a lighthearted congregation of ever-shifting personnel called Dr. Zoom and His Sonic Boom. Dr. Zoom and company weren't so much a band as a traveling bunch of loonies, comic relief set to music to take Asbury Park minds off their problems. Suddenly, everybody had a nickname—Bruce was (naturally) "Dr. Zoom," Vini Lopez became "Mad Dog," Steve Van Zandt was "Miami Steve," and "Southside Johnny" was just that. Through it's brief and notorious career (they *did* open for the Allman Brothers once at the Sunshine Inn), Dr. Zoom and the Sonic Boom had upwards of twenty members, some who could play instruments and some who just played Monopoly on the overflowing stage. There was a Zoom chorus, even some Zoomettes. In short, a lot of fun and not much work.

Next came the Bruce Springsteen Band, which included Mad Dog (the name stuck) Lopez, Miami Steve (ditto), Garry Tallent, and Clarence Clemons. A black ex–football player and a huge talent on saxophone, Clarence quickly became known as "The Big Man." The BSB had up to ten members at one time, including two female singers, but the money made on their occasional gigs couldn't support the group. The lineup kept dwindling, and when Miami split to take a cash gig with oldies band the Dovells (of "Bristol Stomp" fame), it seemed that the carefree Asbury Park scene was coming to an end.

IT'S HARD TO
BE A SAINT IN
THE CITY

Winter in a summer bar-band town takes its toll on musicians. That's when the easygoing groups with no hope or desire for more will break up and go their separate ways. Some of the serious bands, too, will fall. Despite wanting more, and longing for some chance at the brass ring of success, they fall, too. There just isn't much work to be had when the chilly winter air starts closing down the boardwalk bars.

The winter of 1971–72 was rough for Bruce Springsteen. The band bearing his name had dwindled from ten players to seven, to five, and he had decided that it was time to go it alone. His parents were long gone now, and he had just been evicted from the house he grew up in.

He moved in with a friend, Tinker West. They shared a one-room apartment in a makeshift surfboard factory where Bruce got good and depressed and started writing lyrics, which he had never done much before.

Tinker thought some of them were pretty good and introduced Bruce to the only music-biz types he knew—Mike Appel and Jim Cretecos. The team had been co-writers of a Top 40 hit for post-Monkees TV band the Partridge Family. The tune was "Doesn't Somebody Want to Be Wanted," and its million-seller status had enabled the duo to form their own production/management company in Manhattan.

Cretecos and Appel liked Bruce's songs and encouraged him to come up with more. He'd hop a bus into the city from South Jersey and have a new number to show them by the time he arrived at their office. Sometimes, sitting home at the surfboard factory, he'd turn over three songs in a week.

In describing the period to Crawdaddy's Peter Knobler, Bruce said, "I wrote like a madman. Put it out. Had no money, nowhere to go, nothing to do. Didn't know too many people. It was cold and I wrote a lot. And I got to feeling very guilty if I didn't."

Appel and Cretecos didn't take long to realize that they had a talented—and prolific—songwriter on their hands, and in early 1972 Appel offered Bruce a management deal. It was a contract that would later boomerang back to nearly cripple his career, but at the time Bruce thought it was a fine idea. "I had nowhere to go but up," he recalled thinking.

What happened next was one of life's little coincidences that would be hard to believe if you saw it in the movies. Bruce was reading a paperback biography of Bob Dylan and had just finished the part where Dylan walks into the office of Columbia Records' John Hammond, and then walks out with a recording contract. A day after he finished reading that part of the Dylan legend, and three weeks after signing with Appel, Bruce and his guitar were in Hammond's office waiting to see if history would repeat itself.

And it did, although Appel's eagerness almost scotched the deal. As Bruce sat quietly in the corner of Hammond's ten-by-fifteen-foot corner office, Appel was bending Hammond's ear, telling him how lucky he was to hear this boy sing. Hammond, who had been responsible for signing legends like Dylan, Benny Goodman, and Billy Holliday to the label, was not big on being told that *he* was lucky to be there.

Twelve years later, Hammond, whose gracious manners are as legendary as his knack for finding talent, bristles when remembering his first impression of Appel. "The guy was snotty to me," Hammond remembered. "He said he wanted to see if I had any ears, that I was supposed to have discovered Dylan and he had somebody better than Dylan."

Finally, Hammond addressed Bruce himself. "I said, 'I don't want to talk to this character anymore, Bruce, if you'd like to get your guitar out, I'd like to hear what you do.'"

Bruce responded with "It's Hard to Be a Saint in the City," and Hammond forgot all about watching the clock.

"I was supposed to see him for ten minutes and I talked to him for two hours. During this time, I called up the Gaslight [a club] in the Village because I never sign anyone unless I see them perform. Bruce overwhelmed that small audience. There were a couple of good guitar players there and they were asking 'Where did you come up with this guy?' I said 'Oh, he just wandered into my office this morning.'"

Hammond liked Bruce immediately, as both a person—"He, like me, was a devotee of pinball"—and as a performer. "I wrote a little memorandum to CBS saying that I'd heard Bruce and that he was the best artist I'd heard in ten years. I took him into the studio and recorded fourteen tunes immediately, the day after the Gaslight."

Hammond specifically asked that Appel not be present in the studio that day. He and Bruce checked into CBS Studio E, on Fifty-second Street, and worked on some solo audition tapes of Bruce's songs. "On that first audition tape, we did fourteen numbers in two hours," recalled Hammond. "We had a fantastic day recording, including numbers Bruce would never put on wax." There was at least one he would later release as Hammond tells it. "He was on his way to see his girlfriend, off Madison Avenue on 83rd Street, I think it was, and one of the tunes we recorded was 'Does This Bus Stop at 82nd Street?'"

(It wouldn't be until *Nebraska*, ten years later, that Bruce would again record with such startling simplicity. When he was thinking about that album, he called Hammond, with whom he's always stayed in touch, and asked for a copy of his original audition tape. "So I sent him a copy," said Hammond, "and three days later he started recording *Nebraska* the same way.")

Backed with Hammond's recommendation, Bruce was offered his first official recording contract with Columbia Records. In a matter of a few short weeks, he went from being a lonely, struggling young unknown to being John Hammond's new discovery, a pet priority for the Columbia Records sales staff, and the golden hope of label president Clive Davis.

And yet, hard as it is to believe now, there was once a time when you could just walk in off the street and see Bruce Springsteen perform in a club for a mere thirty or forty people. That's exactly how it was in those early days, in New York City, and areas outside of the Asbury Park circuit where Bruce was an established local talent.

If you were enlightened, or just plain lucky enough to stumble into one of these clubs where young Bruce Springstein (a common misspelling) was playing, you'd have seen a live performance quite different from the one Bruce does today.

For instance, it would open with just Bruce, singing solo and playing his acoustic guitar. With his hair cut short and slightly curly and a beard that was still struggling to fill in, you might notice a resemblance to the young Bob Dylan. The Dylan name would echo again when Bruce first started to sing—long, tumbling streams of words, slippery and evocative, flying past almost too quickly. You couldn't quite be sure that they made sense, but they felt right and true and meaningful, and while you watched Bruce's face as he spat out some or lovingly caressed others, there was no doubt about their sincerity. The phrasing—and the words themselves—might change from night to night, but they always resounded with a passion that gave them power and importance.

But wait. Remember, you were in this bar, hearing an unknown guy named Springsteen (or is it Springstein?) play, and you'd just about gotten him pegged as a guitar-strumming singer/songwriter, but maybe with a little more punch. You'd have been wrong again, though, for the E Street band was waiting in the wings.

"All right, let's bring up the band." Bruce would grin, and suddenly the calm would give way to the sight of four psyched-up musicians jumping up to fill in the spaces between the equipment jumbled on the stage. With Garry Tallent on bass, Vini Lopez on drums, Clarence Clemons on sax, and David Sancious on keyboards, Bruce would remove the acoustic and strap on an electric guitar, slung low and menacingly, like a gunslinger's weapon.

Now the songs kicked in harder, the intensity and cutting edge of the lyrics matched by the full, driving power of the band cutting loose. Just as quickly as the band hit that rollicking groove, you would toss aside the folk feelings you had as first impressions. No doubt about it, this Springsteen guy was into rock and roll. And if you were looking around the club and wondering why only thirty-five people stopped in to hear him play, you'd know you were onto something big, something you could tell your friends about in years to come and their eyes would open wide. "You mean you saw Bruce Springsteen play at [local club of your choice]? Sheeeeeeet." If Bruce happened to mention he had an album, *Greetings from Asbury Park, N.J.*, coming out in the next few months, finding it would suddenly become a new priority in your life.

Things had happened quickly and, for the most part, they took Bruce by surprise. Both Hammond and Appel saw Bruce as a solo performer, and neither could understand why he wanted to bring these other guys—rough-looking dudes from New Jersey with names like Vini and Clarence who had no professional recording experience—into the studio. They didn't realize that although Bruce had been alone when they met him, his formative years, earliest influences, and happiest moments had always been with a band.

"I had to fight to get what band there was on there . . ." Bruce would later say of his first album. "Mike didn't know what I was trying to do for at least a year after we were together."

As it was, Bruce didn't know what he wanted to do yet himself, at least as it came to the studio process.

When he and Mike Appel and Jim Cretecos (the latter pair credited as producers) entered 914 Sound Studios in Blauvelt, New York, in June 1972, to begin recording *Greetings from Asbury Park, N.J.*, none of them knew much about how to bring Bruce's rambling musical monologues to life. Appel's only prior production experience was on a pair of LPs for a heavy-metal group, Sir Lord Baltimore. Bruce had nearly total ignorance of the studio which prevented him from pushing forward his ideas. He'd rather ruefully admit when it was over, "That first album, that was sort of out of my control, except for the material. I listen to it, and it sounds real strange to me."

"Madmen, drummers, bummers, and Indians in the summers with a teenage diplomat..." It sounded real strange to a lot of people, the first line from the first track, "Blinded by the Light" of Bruce Springsteen's first album. And it was just the beginning.

In a February 1973 ad to herald the release of *Greetings from Asbury Park, N.J.* Columbia bannered a photo of Bruce (denim work shirt and three-day growth of beard and all) with the claim, "This man puts more thoughts, more ideas, and images into one song than most people put into an album." Between further excerpts from "Blinded," they quoted favorable reviews from Peter Knobler ("There hasn't been an album like this in ages. There are individual lines worth entire records.") and *Record World* magazine ("A completely original vision and a work of genius!") to drive the point home.

Perhaps they were trying *too* hard. Emphasizing Bruce's unique lyrics and the John Hammond audition story, Columbia presented Bruce Springsteen to the world as the new Bob Dylan, as a singer/songwriter who could rival the creator of "Like a Rolling Stone."

It was a common tag thrown on young performers who fit the mold, and one almost guaranteed to annoy radio programmers and music critics, if pushed too far. Perhaps if Bruce had been less talented, the "new Dylan" line would have just gone away, but he *was* a talent—raw and nearly reckless with his wordplay—which made him ripe for a nearly vicious backlash. DJs who saw the Columbia "new Dylan" blurb that was mailed with promotional copies of *Asbury Park* took it as a cue to ignore the LP. The late critic Lester Bangs, with typically maniacal glee, used it as a hook for his *Rolling Stone* review of the LP:

"He's been influenced by the Band, his arrangements tend to take on a Van Morrison tinge every now and then, and he sort of catarrh-mumbles his ditties in a disgruntled mushmouth sorta like Robbie Robertson on Quaaludes with Dylan barfing down the back of his neck." Bruce's wordplay, likewise, was rife for Bangs's blasts: "Some of 'em can mean something socially or otherwise, but there's plenty of 'em that don't even pretend to, reveling in the joy of utter crass showoff talent run amuck and totally out of control."

Bruce remained bemused by all the Dylan comparisons. "The similarities are probably there somewhere. But we come from two totally different scenes..." he told Pat Knight in those early days. "I've been influenced by lots of people. Elvis was one of the first. Otis Redding, Sam Cooke, Wilson Picket, the Beatles, Fats [Domino], Benny Goodman, a lot of jazz guys. You can hear them all in there if you want."

It seemed, however, that nobody wanted to listen. *Greetings* sold fewer than fifty thousand copies in the early months of 1973 and was getting far too little airplay to offer hopes that it might do better. Then, in May, Clive Davis left CBS, and as a result, launching

Bruce Springsteen's career faded in the list of CBS record priorities. As an opening act for Chicago, a ten-piece band then in their glory as jazz-rock hit-makers, Bruce and the E Street Band got a bad taste of the plight of arena support acts. They failed to connect with the audiences they encountered on the Chicago tour and failed again at the July 1973 CBS Records Convention in San Francisco. This was to be Bruce's big chance to prove himself to the collected record company team. The show, however, was a disaster. The band felt ill-at-ease with all the gowns and tuxes watching, and the crowd thought Bruce was cocky and unimpressive.

John Hammond puts it simply: "He laid the biggest egg there ever was. He was nervous, and he was snotty. The crowd was just not very interested in what Bruce had to say, and he was very loud. I went backstage and said, 'Bruce, what do you mean by coming on like an arrogant kid?', and he was just totally embarrassed and said, 'Well, I guess I blew it.'" Columbia seemed to be abandoning Bruce, and the next album would have to be pretty damn good to win them back.

It was! In fact, many Springsteen fans call *The Wild, The Innocent and The E Street Shuffle* Bruce's most underrated album and count it among their favorites of all time.

Bright and playful, full of inspired impishness, tender romance, and hot improvisations, it was described by Bruce himself as "a lazy, hanging-out summer album."

He explained that the feeling was born of the album's circumstances; "That was the summer the band consciousness started to develop," he told *Playboy* magazine. "We were just sitting there flashing on everything that was happening. I was exactly where I wanted to be. I had a band. I knew who I was. We were getting work. The album reflects that."

The word-heavy musings of *Greetings* gave way to a more streamlined sound as Bruce solidified the E Street Band, which now included Danny Federici on organ and various keyboards. The spirit of community within the group stretched out and embraced the songs, too. Bruce was proud to bring out "real warm songs, and a lot of characters.... There was more of a group, a kind of society type feeling. Even if it was low-rent, it was more involvement in groups of people." The cast of characters who inhabit Springsteen's story-song world was growing, but he always insisted they were real. "The stuff I write is what I live with. The stories are all around me. I just put 'em down. They're all true. Even the names, Big Balls Billy, Weak-kneed Willy, all of 'em."

Bruce felt that he was coming into his own as a songwriter, losing the burden of his influences (especially the Dylan tag), and stepping out with his own unique vision. Side two of the album had only three songs—"Incident on 57th Street," "Rosalita," and "New York City Serenade"—but together the trio created a suite, like a rock version of *West Side Story*.

It was a record that had it all—laughs, poignancy, clever lyrics, and great rock—and it went nowhere. The reviews were wonderful—*Rolling Stone* named it one of the best LPs of 1974 (it was actually released in late 1973)—but the sales were dismal. Radio stations still didn't want to play Bruce Springsteen records. Appel, in a fit of pique, sent photocopies of great reviews to many stations with a letter that asked pointedly, "What the hell does it take to get airplay?" The letter was a success in one way—it succeeded in annoying the hell out of many of the program directors who received it.

Columbia was also getting a bit restless. Now that Clive Davis was gone, was there any point in pushing this Springsteen? Even if he got hot, it would just give glory to a boss the company was now trying to forget. It was rumored that without John Hammond and publicist Ron Oberman pleading Springsteen's case, the record company might drop Bruce from the label. "No way," Hammond says now. "I don't really believe there was any question of dropping Bruce. Even the distributers knew he was good."

Bruce was even giving them flack about the kind of concerts they wanted him to do. Still smarting from the Chicago tour, Bruce was refusing to open for bigger acts, and that went against standard operating procedure.

Touring has always been an important and crucial means for musicians—from superstars to unknown garage bands—to support their recorded material. And for young artists especially, it is of major importance in gaining exposure, fans, and, hopefully, airplay. For new performers (even though exposure on MTV has spared many the long haul on the road), touring usually takes on a specific pattern—starting in clubs, then moving on to opening-act status for established stars in big halls, then back down as a headliner to smaller halls (three-thousand seats or so) and college campuses, with hopes of working back up to top of the bill in large halls and arenas. It was a logical and time-tested procedure for the development of new rock acts. And Bruce would have none of it. "I tried playing big halls," he told *The New York Times*. "I couldn't stand it. Everybody was so far away and the band couldn't hear. Maybe if all those people had been there to see me, it would have been different."

His philosophy on the matter was simple. "I did

other things," he said, referring to his few nonmusical jobs. "If you want your house painted green, I paint it green. But when I walk out onstage, I do what *I* want to do."

The results were spectacular—and those who saw him live never forgot, and became loyal fans. Now, if there were just some way of conveying the magic on record. That was the dilemma.

BORN TO RUN

*B*ruce Springsteen's third album was dubbed "long awaited" before he even went into the studio to start recording it. The division that would follow him throughout his career—the battle of "Those Who've Seen Him" and "Those Who Haven't"—had begun. "Those Who Had" were shouting that neither of the first two LPs did Bruce's live act justice. "Those Who Hadn't" were shouting back that no record could justify the kind of wild enthusiasm coming from the other camp.

And whether it was the faith of his followers, or the "show me" burden of his disbelievers, the pressure on Bruce to produce an album worthy of all the shouting was nearly debilitating. They were calling him "the future of rock and roll," for Pete's sake! At least Jon Landau was. A music critic for Boston's *Real Paper* and recordings editor for *Rolling Stone*, Landau had written a glowing review of Springsteen in concert at the Harvard Square Theatre in Cambridge that included the line "I saw rock-and-roll future and its name is Bruce Springsteen." Pulled out of context and repeated endlessly, it was a phrase that would haunt Springsteen for months, *years* to come. When he first heard it, though, it was a welcome bit of praise. "At the time," Bruce remembered, "Landau's quote helped reaffirm a belief in myself. The band and I were making fifty dollars a week. It helped me go on." It also marked the beginning of a friendship between Bruce and Landau that would prove mutually beneficial in ways neither realized when it began.

But in May of 1974, it was, quite simply, put up or shut up time for Bruce, and for a while it looked as if he might actually do the latter. That month, Bruce and Mike Appel headed back into old reliable 914 Studios to begin work on a follow-up to *Wild and Innocent*. Three months later, they emerged with one song, called "Born to Run." Columbia sent an early version of the record to key people in the industry, asking about its possibilities as a single. Most replied that it didn't have a chance—too long, they said. But Appel sent rough mixes to some of the radio stations that had supported Bruce's earlier material. They loved it.

Try as they might, Bruce and Appel couldn't make any progress beyond that one song. Both of them agreed that they shouldn't duplicate the sound of *Greetings* or *Wild and Innocent*, but they seemed doomed to repeat those mistakes unless they could learn some new methods for the studio. Bruce didn't know any shortcuts to get the sound from his head onto vinyl, and the long road was taking its toll. In fact, the frustration was so strong at one point that Bruce threatened to give up making records altogether.

The band was also in a state of flux. In August, David Sancious left the E Street Band to accept a recording contract with Epic Records. Drummer Ernest "Boom" Carter (who had replaced Vini Lopez after the *Wild and Innocent* LP) went with him, and their jazz group, Tone, would record a pair of albums for the label before moving to Arista Records.

It was an amicable split. As David said of his time with Bruce, "We realized from the outset that we had a lot in common and that we could hook up together musically. But we realized that I was going to do my own musical thing eventually and he would continue doing his."

Yet it hurt, nonetheless. "Everybody in the band, we're all friends," David continued, "so there was no graceful way to leave. If you care, it's going to hurt to some degree, no matter how far in advance you know it's going to come."

Springsteen and Appel placed an ad in the *Village Voice*:

Leave Message.
Drummer (No Jr. Ginger Bakers) Piano
(Classical to Jerry Lee Lewis) Trumpet
(Jazz, R&B & Latin) Violin. All must sing.
Male or female. Bruce Springsteen and the E
Street Band. Columbia Records. Call (name
and number) after 12 noon.

Although the band gig offered the unprincely sum of about seventy-five dollars a week, the office was flooded with calls. After auditioning some thirty drummers and thirty keyboard players, Springsteen found a pair of musicians that met his two requirements—they were *good*, and they *wanted* to be in the band.

The drummer, Max Weinberg, was another Jersey boy, with rock bands and a Broadway show in his background. The keyboard player, Roy Bittan, was from Far Rockaway, New York, and had experience in the studio with a number of obscure artists and as a session man. Weinberg was quickly dubbed "Mighty" Max, and Bittan became known as "The Professor" for his well-trained technical chops.

In the fall, violinist Suki Lahav, wife of engineer Louis Lahav, was part of the new lineup temporarily, and by December of 1974, Bruce and company were back in the studio for another month. Still, Bruce couldn't find a unified concept that could embrace all the songs he had written—their various styles and textures just didn't jell. So, in February, the band hit the road again, recording pressure be damned. As Bruce said at the time, "I just don't work on a deadline or anything like that. If I'm gonna do this, it's gonna be fun."

While the road was fun, it was also ultimately a boost to the album's progress. Removed from the studio, where every take had to be perfect, and set loose in front of a crowd, Roy and Max settled into the E Street Band. Each night they got looser in spirit, tighter with the other players, and felt freer to add their input to the developing material. The songs themselves came into sharper focus as live audiences gave their immediate feedback on what worked and what didn't.

In a live radio broadcast from Philadelphia's Main Point in early 1975, one could hear the changing nature of the songs that would later appear on *Born to Run*. Typically, when offered a chance to solidify his audience at a crucial point in his career, Bruce chose to test out new variations on his material rather than go for the tried and true.

"Born to Run" was essentially unchanged at this point, but "Thunder Road" is a telling example of how vulnerable the material was at the time. In its Main Point performance, the song did not even have its title chorus—Bruce fairly mumbled "dance all the way" or "take a chance" in the spaces where the words "Thunder Road" would later fit. Nearly half of the song's lyrics would be rewritten by the time of its recording—the name of the girl on the porch would change from Angelina to Mary (she was also Christy in another version), and simplistic lines like "make up your mind girl, I gotta get her back out on the street" gave rise to the poetry of "make crosses from your lovers, throw roses in the rain." The song would undergo some musical revisions as well. "Thunder Road" ended in those days with a violin passage beneath the final verse and a bouncy, cha-cha-flavored sax riff from Clarence before the final instrumental build. All told, an interesting number, but a pale comparison to the aching beauty of the finished tune.

"She's the One" appeared musically solid but displayed an edge of violence in this earlier incarnation, with references to girls that "wanna rip her apart" and "getting beat" in the streets of New York. A couplet about going to the movies and trying to walk like the heroes seen on the screen would later be moved to "Backstreets." Like "Thunder Road," more than half of the song's lyrics would be changed in the studio.

Finally, there is "Jungleland," whose minor lyrical modifications would not be half as important as two key musical changes. First, and almost incomprehensible given its now-classic status, there was *no* Clarence Clemons sax solo in this version. Instead, Bruce was trying to achieve the climactic build to the story of the two young lovers through a traditional guitar solo. And equally conspicuous by its absence is the final, tortured vocal howl from Bruce that stands as the song's stirring coda. To anyone hearing the *Born to Run* material in these early months of 1975, it was clear that the album had the potential to be a classic, yet still had a long way to go.

It was obvious that the project of recording Bruce's third album, having dragged on for nearly a year, needed a boot in the butt. Although Jon Landau had limited production experience—with the MC5 and with Livingston Taylor—Bruce thought he might fit the bill based on personal chemistry. Since the "future of rock" review, Bruce had stayed in touch with the supportive critic, and frequently crashed at Landau's Manhattan apartment on those nights when he missed the last bus to Jersey.

Bruce had asked Landau to sit in on one of the sessions at 914 Studios in February and liked the writer's ability to pinpoint problems in the recording process. Some weeks later, Landau sat in again at a late night mixing session of "Born to Run," and Bruce invited himself to Landau's apartment afterward. Over a late-night snack, Bruce asked Jon to help out on the LP. In explaining his reasons for choosing Jon, Bruce recalled that "whenever we'd talk, he'd have something important to tell me. It became obvious that I needed somebody with this outside perspective."

Landau was interested, but cautious. A few weeks later, he came to a band rehearsal in New Jersey, and this time it was he who crashed in Bruce's place. The next day, Bruce confessed that he had obtained Landau's bed—a ratty old couch—from a neighbor's garbage. Despite the accommodations, Landau, after a successful rehearsal session, agreed to coproduce the album with Appel and Bruce. He quit his job and the three got to work.

Landau's positive impact on the recording was immediately apparent. After one session at 914, he convinced Appel to move out of the decaying studios (the phones didn't even work!) and spring the extra money to move the action into Manhattan's Record Plant studio. He hired a young engineer named Jimmy Iovine, a veteran of sessions with John Lennon and Phil Spector (who would later go on to be a successful producer himself for Stevie Nicks and Tom Petty, among others).

But perhaps most important, Landau lit a new spark in Bruce's creativity and enthusiasm. A perfectionist who couldn't stop—or didn't dare to—when revising his material, Bruce was always looking for one more way to play a song. As long as the possibility of a different way, a better way, existed, he couldn't let go. As Landau put it, "The indecision comes from fear. If you do one thing, that means you can't do another. Bruce wants it all. He always wants it all." And despite attempts not to think about the pressure, Bruce knew that this record would be under heavy-duty scrutiny. Landau told the *Village Voice*, "The biggest thing I learned from him was the ability to concentrate on the big picture. 'Hey, wait a second,' he would say. 'The release date is just one day, but the record is forever.'"

Landau convinced Bruce that to put off the record any longer was not to do right by the fans, or by himself. Yes, it was important to do the thing right, but it was even more important to *do it*.

Once Landau was aboard, the work proceeded at an exhausting pace. Prior to his appearance, there was only one song on tape and a few others written. With

Landau, "Thunder Road" came together relatively quickly. When Bruce saw how he could bring a tune to fruition in a matter of days, he was so excited that he finished writing the rest of the songs in a matter of three weeks.

Even so, Bruce would later describe the period spent cutting that album as one of the worst times of his life. "It was like a monster let loose. It wanted everything. It just ate up everybody's life."

Near the end of the exhausting schedule, it was not unusual for Bruce to have three Record Plant studios in action at one time—a vocal track being recorded here, mixing over there, a band rehearsal in yet another. "By the time the mixes came around, I was beat to a pulp," he said. And though the band was up to the task and supportive of each other, "Some days when you got in there, it was like murder. Some of the stuff that was in the air in that studio was *deadly*." Bruce was able to laugh when it was all over. "People would *back off* . . .!"

The day the *Born to Run* tracks were finally finished, in July 1975, Bruce played a live gig in Providence, Rhode Island. He'd had an eleventh-hour thought to scrap the record and just record an upcoming week of Bottom Line (NYC) live shows, but he ultimately agreed to go with the record as it was. He admitted to finding *Born to Run* "a scary album," with its full, booming mix, and took with a grain of salt all the talk about it being the long-awaited Big One.

"It's a waste of time worrying about whether you're gonna be a big star or a small star," Bruce told writer David Fandray. "It's out of your hands. You just do what you do."

So Bruce settled into his newly rented home overlooking Manhattan from the Jersey cliffs and tooled around town in his new toy, a '57 Chevy. The record was finished, and he was happy. All the talk that had surrounded the first two albums hadn't amounted to much. Why would this one be any different?

He obviously wasn't thinking about the Columbia Records promotion machine.

BLINDED BY THE LIGHT

"Tell your papa I ain't no freak, 'cause now I got
my picture, Rosie, on the cover of *Time* and
Newsweek!"

—Bruce Springsteen, in concert
performances of "Rosalita," 1975

*A*s early as June 1975,
while Bruce was still in the studio, *Born to Run* became
a hot project at Columbia records. Some execs heard
a rough mix of the title track and decided to sink more
money into the promotion of Mr. Springsteen. They
revived the Landau quote, made allusions to the album
that was on the way, and pushed again in print on
behalf of Bruce's first two records. As a result, *Greetings* and *Wild and Innocent* doubled their original sales,
and advance orders for *Born to Run* were higher than
anything Bruce had ever known before. In Washington, D.C., a "Springsteen city," advance orders were
triple that of Elton John's then-current LP.

The same promo folks who couldn't spell Springsteen's name two years ago suddenly had him on priority lists. The pressing plants and media machines would
be put on overdrive for this one.

None of which would have made any difference if

Bruce and his music couldn't click with the public. But
it could, and it was doing so in a big way months before
the album's release. Despite its four-and-a-half-minute
length, the "Born to Run" single was getting major
airplay and climbing the charts steadily. It was Bruce's
first hit single ever and made it to the Top Forty.

A five-night stand (August 13–17) at Manhattan's
Bottom Line club was a summer smash and a high
point for Bruce. It was the inauguration of his first
national tour and, maybe even better, marked the end
of the *Born to Run* recording saga—the final mixes
were approved just before the concerts. Out of four
thousand tickets available for the ten-show appearance, Columbia bought nearly one thousand to give
members of the press. Like any true Springsteen fans,
they worked on a simple principle—get the bodies in
the hall and Bruce will do the rest.

The shows were *hot*—fans lined the streets sur-
rounding the Greenwich Village club, desperately
jockeying for the chance to buy the few standing-
room-only tickets available for each night's show.
WNEW-FM, New York's premier progressive rock
station at the time, broadcast the August 15 show live
to the New York metropolitan region and helped spread
the word.

That same August day, *New York Times* music critic
John Rockwell told the world in print, "Mr. Springsteen has it all—he is a great lyricist and songwriter,
guitarist and piano player, he has one of the best rock
bands anybody has ever heard, and he is as charismatic
a stage figure as rock has produced."

As soon as Bruce strutted on stage in white T-shirt,
blue jeans, black leather jacket, and tweed cap, the
crowd knew they were in for an evening of rock they

would always remember. From the opening swagger of "Tenth Avenue Freeze-Out" (once more, he went for a new song instead of the tried and true) until the knockout encore punch of Gary U.S. Bonds's "Quarter to Three," Bruce lived up to all the superlatives of Rockwell's review.

That the live shows were so spectacular should have come as no surprise—Bruce and the band were damn glad to be out of the studio and back in front of the crowd. The studio had always felt like someone else's home ground, a place that constantly demanded that you prove yourself. But Bruce could step out on any stage and feel totally in control. The stage was *his* turf, and he was glad to be prowling it again. Miami Steve Van Zandt was now officially ensconced as new guitarist for the E Street Band (the Bottom Line shows were his public debut) and Bruce virtually put down his guitar to concentrate on other stage matters. For instance, in "Spirit in the Night" he literally crawled out onto the tables of the four-hundred-seat club and snuggled up to one (presumably still-shocked) female for the "me and crazy Janey were making love in the dirt" passage. Then it was back to the stage to rediscover the magic of the Crystals's oldie "Then She Kissed Me," a few numbers from the first two discs, and then another oldie (the Searchers's "When You Walk in the Room") before getting down to *Born to Run* previews.

There was none of the Main Point performance's tentativeness here—"She's the One," "Born to Run," and "Thunder Road" were now finished works, with each word just where it should be. Yet, as is his wont, Bruce would play with the texture of the songs in concert—"Thunder Road" was performed as a solo piece on the piano. Sung slow and tender, the song moved with the quiet grace of Mary's dress waving in the wind and is perhaps Bruce's most touching love song ever.

The fans were ecstatic, the critics effusive. "Springsteen fashions the kind of seamless, 150-minute performance that most artists can only dream about, never realize," wrote Paul Nelson in the *Village Voice*. "On my feet, clapping, never wanting it to end, I ask myself when I've ever been so moved by a concert." Dave Herman of WNEW-FM went on the air the next day to publicly apologize for not having played more Springsteen material in the past.

Even Bruce, his own harshest critic, was pleased with the week's run of shows. "There's nothin'— nothin'—in the world to get you playin' better than a gig like that. The band walked out of the Bottom Line twice as good as when they walked in," he said happily.

With the E Street Band playin' like "the finest machine there was," in Bruce's words, they hit the road on September, 1975, and stayed on it until a New Year's Eve farewell in Philly. At the Roxy, a Los Angeles showcase theater similar to the Bottom Line, a celebrity-studded crowd (Jack Nicholson, Nils Lofgren, Ryan and Tatum O'Neal, Neil Diamond, Joni Mitchell, and others) stood on their chairs and screamed their approval. A week later, in Red Bank, New Jersey, a movie marquee read simply "Homecoming," but everyone knew just who it was for.

By the time *Born to Run* was actually released, in October, Springsteen fever had reached epidemic proportions. Greil Marcus, in the October 9, 1975, *Rolling Stone* record review section (sixty-five pages after a glowing feature by John Rockwell) called *Born to Run* "a magnificent album that pays off on every bet ever placed on him—a '57 Chevy running on melted down Crystals records that shuts down every claim that has been made. And it should crack his future wide open."

Stereo Review said, "If you've ever believed in rock 'n' roll, then you absolutely have to have *Born to Run*." Enough people took the advice to make *Born to Run* a gold record within weeks of its release.

At a time when rock music was being threatened by the martial beat of the disco drums, the rock press made it seem as if Bruce Springsteen had single-handedly (well, the E Street Band certainly helped) resurrected rock. Also, at a time when "faceless," relatively bland personalities dominated the music scene, Bruce had an image that was perfect for the papers.

The cocky assurance that Bruce emitted onstage turned to quiet charisma when he stepped off. Speaking slowly, struggling for just the right words and peppering "ya knows" in his conversation, he might strike you at first as inarticulate, but then he'd throw in a zinger, brown eyes flashing, that buried that impression once and for all. He had a colorful past full of exotic characters, and a burning passion for rock that was both unfashionably sentimental and endearingly sincere. His physical appearance worked, too—looking like a cross between a sensitive beatnik and a punkish backstreet hood made for great photos.

Mike Appel started doing what he did best—pushing for his star act. The demand for Springsteen interviews was so strong that Appel limited them to only those publications that would put Bruce on the cover. (*Playboy* was the only one that managed to get him otherwise.) Columbia Records, meanwhile, sank nearly $250,000 into promotion for the record.

Bruce was aware that the stakes had suddenly become much higher in his career. "You know, things've gotten heavier lately," he told *Crawdaddy* in October of 1975. "It's like you could *feel* things getting heavier.

At the record company. In the band. All over. Doesn't seem like anything in particular, just things starting to weigh in."

And some would tip the scales against him. Just like the "new Dylan" backlash that hounded the *Greetings* album, there were those who said all this praise of Springsteen was no more than record company hype. In the October 5, 1975, Sunday edition of the *New York Times*, critic Henry Edwards declared, "If there hadn't been a Bruce Springsteen, then the critics would have made him up." He went on to dismiss Bruce's lyrics, melodies, and stage show and concluded, "Given such flaws, there had to be another important ingredient to the success of Bruce Springsteen: vigorous promotion."

Most of the music industry took Edwards's attack less than seriously. It was a great way to stir up controversy, but not particularly relevant. In his career up to this point, Bruce had gone against the grain of most standard promotional methods, had done things in his own way, and had the kind of fanatical audience that no amount of record company money could buy.

But Edwards's column got other non-music-oriented magazines interested in this "new pop star," and in the last week of October 1975, Bruce Springsteen inadvertantly achieved a feat that no rocker had done before. He was the cover story for national news weeklies *Time* and *Newsweek* simultaneously. Being on the cover of either publication was considered a coup for any public figure. Being on both at the same time was unheard of for a rock performer, and caused even more of a Springsteen sensation.

Bruce recalled the whole incident with a laugh. "It was like, now who would believe this? Would you look at *this*? But my father said, 'Why not you? Better you than another picture of the President.'"

Miami Steve was laughing too. The morning, after the magazines appeared on the stands, he told *Playboy*, "Now it's gonna get worse with these two stories. Everybody's gonna be asking us what it's like to be a phenomenon. I don't even know how to spell the word. Is that with a P or F?"

"What phenomenon? What phenomenon?" *Newsweek* had already quoted Bruce. "We're driving around, and we ain't no phenomenon. The hype just gets in the way. People have gone nuts. It's weird. All the stuff you dream about is there, but it gets diluted by all the other stuff that jumped on you by surprise."

The two articles were quite different. *Newsweek* called theirs "Making of a Rock Star" and directly addressed the possibility of hype at work. "Some people are asking," they wrote, "whether Bruce Springsteen will be the biggest superstar or the biggest hype of the seventies."

The *Time* article was more supportive, treating Bruce as a legitimate rock star and calling the "hype" a natural consequence of his special talents.

Still, all this noise and hoopla didn't seem quite fair to Bruce. Expectations seemed to follow him everywhere he went. First it was the burden of recording *Born to Run*, and now this media bandwagon thing, attempting to somehow minimize the quality of his work, the justice of his success. Though he tried, it must have been nearly impossible for Bruce to keep his distance from it all.

When the E Street Band headed to Europe in November 1975 for a brief tour of England and Holland, the overseas critics were so full of advance stories about Springsteen that they, too, turned against him. Walking into the lobby of a London theater to make his U.K. debut, Bruce was astonished to find the walls plastered with posters shouting, "At last London is ready for Bruce Springsteen!" In a rare fit of anger, he personally ripped them down.

Los Angeles critic Robert Hilburn wrote of this time in Springsteen's career: "I just hope he's strong enough to stand up under the pressure." Neither of them could have known at the time just how prophetic that statement would be.

BADLANDS

"1976 is the year of Bruce Springsteen—why wait?"
—British CBS Records ad

"When you make more than $500 a night, you get
more than $500 problems."
—Bruce Springsteen, 1978

Hype or no hype, Bruce Springsteen's career had hit its stride, and it looked as if the only way to go from here was up. As 1976 opened, there was plenty of activity in the Springsteen camp.

Miami Steve had gone into the studio with his old buddies Southside Johnny and the Asbury Jukes to produce their debut LP for Epic Records. Bruce wrote the liner notes for the record, bringing back old stories of the Upstage Club days, and described Southside as "the only white kid on the Jersey Shore that you could stand to hear sing straight R&B five sets a night." Two Springsteen originals—"The Fever" (a 1973 studio track that Bruce recorded but never released) and "You Mean So Much to Me" (an ode to the Phil Spector days that Johnny did as a duet with Ronnie Spector)—also appeared on the LP, titled *I Don't Want to Go Home*. It sold well for a debut album and launched yet another

Asbury Park band into the national scene.

Meanwhile, Jon Landau was in Los Angeles, working on tracks for Jackson Browne's next LP, *The Pretender*, and then plans were made for him and Bruce to begin *Born to Run*'s follow-up sometime in the summer. Springsteen would relax on the East Coast in the interim and work out some contractual details with Mike Appel.

Or so he thought. What followed was a classic case of a naive young performer learning the hard way about the meaning of money and the legal machine in the music business.

Bruce has always admitted freely and openly that he cared nothing about the money that his music brought him. "If they had told me I was the janitor and would have to mop up and clean the toilets after the show in order to play, I probably would have done it," he told rock journalist Lisa Robinson. Now he *was* making good money, and oddly enough that seemed to be worse than not making it.

"Before *Born to Run* it was different," he told *Good Times*'s David Fandray. "We were young, we were running around the country, we were staying anyplace we could. There was money comin' and going out. Like nobody had money, but all I know is you had money in your pocket, and before then you didn't have money in your pocket. So, life was great.

"Then, *Born to Run* hit and it was a big success and all of a sudden there was more money than could be spent. *This* was a problem. This means there's money here, so whose is it? That was where all the trouble started. Oh God! Everyone has an idea how much is theirs, how much is the other guy's."

One of these people, naturally enough, was Bruce's original manager and producer, Mike Appel. Appel had always been a tough negotiator and pitchman, and, though a certain amount of aggressiveness is important to any success in the highly competitive music industry, there were those who said that Appel's technique was too abrasive. He was Bruce's champion, all right, and he had been responsible for getting the Hammond audition and Columbia recording deal. But he had also alienated many people along the way. A question hung in the air—was Appel looking out for Springsteen's best interests?

Typically, Bruce did not like to think badly about someone he considered a friend. Yes, he and Mike had had their disagreements: Mike wanted to book the E Street Band into large halls and stadiums, which went against Bruce's vision of the live show; Mike wanted to release live tapes as the next LP, but Bruce wanted to wait on that score and make a studio LP for his fourth release. These disagreements, however, did not change the basic fact that Mike had offered Bruce his first shot at the big time. Mike had been with him in the beginning, and it seemed only right that he should be with Bruce now.

Supposedly, Appel offered Springsteen a chance to renegotiate their original contracts, but Bruce responded that he'd just as soon proceed on a day-to-day verbal agreement that reflected his trust. Appel wasn't pleased with that idea, and his reaction caused Bruce to wonder just what *was* in his original contracts with Appel.

On a visit to California, Bruce asked Jon Landau to look at the papers. His friend's reply was that Bruce would need a lawyer. The contracts, still valid between Bruce and Appel, seemed highly disadvantageous to the performer.

As it stood, Bruce had three contracts with Appel—

one for management, one for recording, and one for publishing. Appel, in effect, had control of the major part of Bruce's creative efforts.

According to *Rolling Stone* magazine, an audit showed that while Bruce was getting about eighteen cents for each record he sold, Appel's company was getting about forty cents. Being both Bruce's manager *and* head of the production company that made Bruce's records could even put Appel in the unique position of negotiating with himself for Bruce's services. The contracts forbade this but also forbade Bruce from having any other advisors besides Appel. The result was that when it was time to enter the studio, Bruce (the total nonbusinessman) had to consider Appel's terms (and he was a professional businessman) without any outside counsel.

The thing that hurt the most was Bruce's realization that he did not control the use of his own songs. Appel's publishing company controlled them and could, if they liked, forbid even Bruce from quoting them. This, to Bruce, was the last straw. On July 27, 1976, his lawyers filed suit against Appel in federal court, attempting to void all contracts with Appel based on charges of fraud, breach of trust, misappropriation of funds, and false representation. In short, it was charged that Appel was making deals that worked to his own benefit and not Bruce's.

Appel's company promptly countered the suit with one of its own. Appel asked the court to forbid Bruce from going into the studio with Landau to record any material until the case was settled. Appel charged that Landau had engaged in a "campaign to sabotage the relations between Springsteen and myself." Naturally, Bruce wanted Landau to produce his next album—the two had grown close during the recording of *Born to Run*. Landau had helped him record his biggest success to date after a long, less productive period with Appel at the console. But Appel was opposed to—some would say jealous of—Landau's growing influence and friendship with Bruce. Certainly, it didn't help when the infamous *Newsweek* cover story ran a photo that was captioned: "Springsteen, manager Landau, girlfriend Darbin."

According to part of Appel's management contract with Bruce, Appel had the right to refuse approval of any producer, and he was now putting it in effect with regard to Landau.

The court came down in support of Appel's existing contracts, so Bruce and Landau were forbidden to work together at a crucial time in Bruce's career. His future was put in the hands of men in three-piece suits, and for Bruce, who had spent his whole life fighting back at authority, this was a cruel and cutting irony. He had become just what he wanted to be—a rock 'n' roller—and now a group of strangers was going to decide how, when, and with whom he could record his music.

Since Appel's company had received a healthy advance from Columbia after *Born to Run*'s release, he could afford to wait out the court battle. But Bruce had to make money to keep himself and the band going. He needed an outlet, too, for his creative energies, so the E Street Band hit the road again. First, he toured the South for two months, and then broke for the summer to shave off his beard and play a week of shows in Red Bank, New Jersey. Fall brought with it his first arena dates as a headliner, including the 7,500-seat Phoenix Coliseum. He was reluctant at first to attempt such a large venue, but played longer and harder than ever to give fans their money's worth. He also instituted an exhausting four-hour soundcheck to ensure that the cavernous arena had the best possible sound for his fans. The system worked, and this laid the groundwork for the massive tours awaiting him.

What he couldn't do in the studio, Bruce now did on stage, testing new material and sifting through old favorites for inspiration. The Animals' "It's My Life" became a heartrending live number, especially as it opened with the searing solioquy in which Bruce described the fights he'd had with his dad when he was much younger. Another lighter rap evolved for the middle section of "Growin' Up," and there was a new pop number called "Rendezvous". Other songs pegged for the next album, whenever it might be, showed a darker side. "The Promise" (which never officially made it to vinyl) was a brooding tune about "broken promises and cashed-in dreams" that many listeners interpreted as a direct comment on the court proceedings. (In fact, Bruce would drop it from the next LP for that very reason. "I don't write songs about lawsuits," he said simply.) And "Something in the Night," which *would* see release, was sometimes embellished with a melancholy trumpet line borrowed from the Jukes' Miami Horns.

When not on the road, Bruce donned an unfamilar jacket and tie and stood in court, giving depositions in hopes of gaining his freedom from the Appel contracts. He described the process sadly to *Crawdaddy*'s Peter Knobler, admitting that it was an ugly scene. "But, on the other hand, it's still a guy that you . . . kinda . . . like, and you know he . . . kinda . . . likes you." In the years to come, Bruce would never publicly disavow Mike Appel. "When we started," he told *SOUNDS* magazine, "Mike was as naive as me in a certain way—it was like he'd be the Colonel and I'd be Elvis, except that he wasn't the Colonel and I wasn't Elvis. That was our story. I just wanted myself back again."

It took a long time. At first, Bruce's court appearances were near disasters. Ill at ease and unused to the legalities involved, his depositions were awkward and possibly damaging to his cause. But as Bruce took to heart the idea that he was fighting for his life, he got tough. ("That's why I started playing music in the first place—to control my life. No way I was gonna let that get away.") His depositions were never made public, but some who heard them said that his later speeches before the court were as impassioned and dramatic as his best live performances. Bruce helped turn the case around by showing just how sincere he was in wanting his creative work restored to him.

Bruce felt he was losing valuable time, and his songwriter's spark. In an affadavit sworn on December 8, 1976, he said: "Ever since the issuance of the court's preliminary injunction order, I have started countless numbers of songs which I have been unable to develop to their potential for lack of a proper recording opportunity. . . . Many of these songs will never be finished."

He also stressed the importance of working with Landau, saying, "Landau has brought to the studio higher qualities which have given tremendous stride to my creative development. . . . Laudau's ability to communicate with me stems from the simple fact that I trust him."

And finally, he made clear his personal bottom line: "[Appel's] interest in this action is strictly financial," he said in closing. "My interest is my career, which up until now holds the promise of my being able to significantly contribute to, and possibly influence, a generation of music. No amount of money could compensate me if I were to lose this opportunity."

On May 28, 1977, at three A.M., the court finally settled the conflict between Springsteen and Appel by dissolving the relationship. Both sides felt victorious. Appel got a large financial settlement and a share of the profits from the first three Springsteen LPs. Bruce saw all three of his contracts with Appel rescinded, and was free to go into the studio with whomever he liked. And, most importantly, whatever songs he recorded there would be *his*.

On June 1, 1977, a year after their initial appointment to meet, Bruce and Jon Landau entered Atlantic studios in New York City to begin work on the next Springsteen LP.

DARKNESS ON THE EDGE OF TOWN

*A*lthough it felt good to be back in the studio, during that June of 1977 Springsteen and Landau had their work cut out for them, even with help from their friends. Miami Steve was now credited for production assistance, and Jimmy Iovine was back behind the console to record the proceedings. The action would run through eleven months and some thirty songs before Bruce had the album down to his satisfaction. "I wanted to learn," he said upon emerging from the studio, "so I wanted to take my time."

If anybody thought that time was spent leisurely, Max Weinberg would tell them otherwise: "Nobody, except the people who were there, will know how hard Bruce worked on *Darkness*. He just drove himself...on and on...." For most of the year, Bruce, with and without the band, was in the studio fifteen hours a day, five days a week.

The first question was one of song selection. In the period since finishing *Born to Run*, he had dozens. There were so many songs available for the album that rumor had it this might be a double, even triple, LP. In reality, only thirteen songs were planned for actual release.

There was also a full LP's worth of pop songs done in the style of the early English invasion that had so inspired Bruce's youth. "But I didn't feel it was the right time to do that," he later told writer Dave Marsh, "and I didn't want to sacrifice any of the intensity of the album by throwing in 'Rendezvous,' even though I knew it was popular from the show."

He was referring to a wonderful pop tune that ultimately went to the Greg Kihn Band, a quartet of journeyman rockers who were very big in the San Francisco area (and would become successful with "Jeopardy"). Many of the other *Darkness* tunes were also given away to other rock 'n' rollers—"Hearts of Stone" and "Talk to Me" became highlights of the Asbury Jukes' third LP for Epic Records; Robert Gordon got "Fire" (later a hit for the Pointer Sisters); and Patti Smith earned her first Top 40 single with "Because the Night," which she coauthored with Bruce. There were other tunes that fell through the cracks—like "Outside Looking In," a number with the rolling Buddy Holly drum sound used in "She's the One," as well as "Don't Look Back," a title that was pulled off the disc so late that it even appeared in a record store catalogue of new releases. And "Independence Day" would have to wait for the next record.

Bruce was cutting down on the lengthy songs like "Backstreets" and "Jungleland" and moving toward a more distilled, compact type of material. He was stripping down the tumble of words that infused tracks like

"Tenth Avenue Freeze-Out," but as any writer knows, sometimes it's harder to edit complex thoughts than to let them have their lead and expand.

The reckless romanticism of *Born to Run* was giving way to a harsher reality. Mary, the girl on the porch in "Thunder Road," was now sitting there alone in "Racing in the Street" while her man tried to relieve his numbness in drag competitions. The link between the two numbers would be emphasized in concert when Bruce segued the newer tune back to the older one with a mournful harmonica solo.

"This record, I think it's less romantic," Bruce explained to the *Memphis Commercial Appeal*. "It's got more, a little more isolation. It's sort of like, I said, 'Well, I'm twenty-eight years old and the people in the album are around my age.' I perceive them to be that old and they don't know what to do. They're trying to figure out what to do.... There's less of a sense of a free ride in *Darkness* than in *Born to Run*. There's more a sense of: if you wanna ride, you're gonna pay, and you better keep riding. There's just a little more world awareness."

Bruce was telling a new story on this album, one that reflected the hard lessons he'd learned in the past year. Still, his themes continued to involve cars, the highway, and life on the street. "My stuff is like these Italian western movies," he'd say of the recurring topics. "I write particular types of songs—using the same imagery—but what happens to the characters is different." On *Darkness*, quite simply, Bruce's characters were growing up.

So was the band, working in subtly shifting sonic textures. Clarence's saxophone was used more sparingly on the album than on previous releases, down to only three of the ten songs, while Bruce's guitar came up to the forefront. With echoes of Jimmy Page, Jeff Beck, and even Hendrix, Bruce's guitar roared on a cutting edge, slicing sharply through the material to give it a ragged edge of danger. His solo leads screamed in the best tradition of Clapton and Townshend. "A lot of the songs were not really suited to the saxophone," Bruce explained. "The sax is a very warm instrument and the songs have a bit more detachment, more of a hard edge, they're cooler, and more suited to the guitar."

Danny Federici's organ playing was also brought up, while Max Weinberg's drumming kicked in with a booming bass wallop in the final mix.

At first, production proceeded with a mind toward achieving a layered sound similar to *Born to Run*, and Columbia was hoping that the record would be ready for a Christmas 1977 release. In the fall, though, Bruce decided he wanted a more "live" sound, and the E Street Band rerecorded many of the tracks live in the studio. "Streets of Fire" and "Something in the Night," as they eventually appeared on vinyl were both first takes, in fact.

Even the name of the record would change. At one point, flipping through an index of movie titles in an encyclopedia of American cinema, Bruce took a liking to the words "American Madness" and considered that for the album's name. He was becoming very interested in film during the recording of the LP, citing *The Grapes of Wrath* as a strong influence on the album's development and themes. But *Darkness on the Edge of Town* it would be.

It would also be one of the most eagerly awaited albums of the year.

In April of 1978, Bruce was telling anxious reporters and record execs that the album had "just a few touches

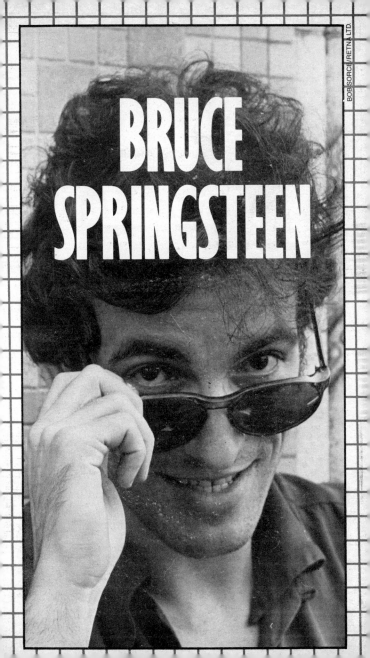

BRUCE
SPRINGSTEEN

A pensive Bruce. In 1977, at left, and in the fall of 1982, above, around the time of Nebraska's release.

BOB GRUEN/STAR FILE

A man with a mike—Bruce giving his fans a from-the-heart performance.

MICHAEL PUTLAND/RETNA, LTD.

ANASTASIA PANTSIOS/STAR FILE

ANASTASIA PANTSIOS/STAR FILE

How the Boss
looks onstage—
way to go, Bruce!

*F*eeling the muse. As one review said, "If you've ever believed in rock 'n' roll, then you absolutely have to have Born to Run."

JANET MACOSKA/STAR FILE

Whether in an earlier incarnation in baggy trousers or his familiar faded denims, Bruce is a mesmerizing figure when he performs.

*H*e can rock in a shirt 'n' tie or stroll in a cutoff T and shades— there's only one Bruce Springsteen.

FELIX PHOTOGRAPHY/B. L. HOWARD PRODUCTIONS, LTD.

Clarence Clemons letting it rip, at right. Below: Fans awaiting a Bruce Benediction. Opposite page: Bruce outside the New Jersey factory where his father had worked.

ANASTASIA PANTSIOS/STAR FILE

*T*he E Street Band. At top: New members on the 1984–85 World Tour, guitarist Nils Lofgren (who replaced "Miami" Steve) and singer Patty Scialfa. Below, left to right: Clarence, Bruce, "Miami" Steve, Danny, Garry, Max, and Roy.

JANET MACOSKA/STAR FILE

JAMES SHIVE/RETNA LTD.

Above left: Bruce, manager Jon Landau, and Jackson Browne leaving the stage after Bruce's surprise performance with Browne at the Central Park rally for Nuclear Disarmament in 1982. Left: The joint was jumping as over 1,000 lucky fans saw Bruce at the Stone Pony warmup gig for the 1984–85 tour.

left" and that it would be out "real soon." But, as always, he would not let go of it one moment before it was ready.

He even got involved in the printing process for the cover shot. While a dramatic portrait of Bruce on the desert was originally pegged for the album jacket, Bruce decided he wanted something less posed. Patti Smith suggested that an old college friend of hers, Frank Stefanko, a meatpacker from South Jersey with free-lance photography credits, would fit the bill. So Bruce drove over to Stefanko's house, and they talked for hours in the kitchen, Bruce explaining the tone of the record. When they were done, they wandered through the house, looking for a suitable setting, and found it in an upstairs bedroom, in front of a window with drawn blinds. "I can't put it in words exactly," said Stefanko, "but suddenly he reminded me of myself at age fourteen. It was something in his face." The determined face—now clean-shaven—that stared out quietly from the cover of *Darkness* seemed entirely appropriate for the new maturity of the sounds within.

While Bruce oversaw finishing touches, Columbia placed *Darkness* in its "immediate special" category, meaning that as soon as the master was presented to the company it would be prepared for rush release. They, like all the anxious disc jockeys and fans, wanted the record in their hands as soon as it was humanly possible.

The desire to be the first with the disc became almost comical. With all the radio stations scrambling for an advance tape, and Columbia fighting them off until the official release date, a number of mistakenly labeled copies of *Darkness* appeared in a New Jersey record store in Barbra Streisand *Songbird* covers. The error was discovered when a Springsteen fan overheard a Streisand fan complaining to a record store cashier that her *Songbird* rocked too hard. Realizing the situation, the delighted fan offered to buy the record, and was thus able to leak a legally purchased advance copy of *Darkness* to a grateful WNEW-FM.

When the rest of the rock world heard the record, they were shocked and, for the most part, pleased. It was a tough, no-punches-pulled album that demanded attention—and got it in spades. Many critics felt that the album might even surpass *Born to Run* as Bruce's definitive statement.

New Musical Express, the British music weekly, said: "Bruce's back, after years in the litigation wilderness, with his *Darkness on the Edge of Town* album which, while nowhere near as instantly habit-forming as *Born to Run*, reveals itself soon enough as the most intrinsically powerful work with added depth, maturity, and *soul*."

J. M. DeMatteis, of Long Island's *Good Times*, put it this way: "*Born to Run* is more exhilarating, *E Street* is more fun, but this album is brutal, unrelenting, and painfully honest—a revealing trip through the tunnel of the soul to the light on the other side."

Naturally, there were those who disagreed. Some cited Bruce's repetitions of the car/highway/street subject matter as a sign of stagnation, or found the brooding intensity too melodramatic. *Creem*'s Mitch Cohen, while crediting the record for being "passionate" and "artful," said he would gladly "trade all seven minutes of 'Racing in the Streets,' including Roy Bittan's admirable piano work, for one moment of the spontaneity with which Bruce shouts, 'Come on Wendy!' like some hoodlum Peter Pan in 'Born to Run.'" And even Bruce's fiercest fans could find some humor in Cohen's rhetorical question "Doesn't this guy ever get in the car just to get a pack of cigarettes? It's a major production every time he turns the ignition key."

If any criticism of the record bothered Bruce himself, it was the idea that *Darkness* was a depressing album, or one whose theme was despair. "*Darkness* is about *dealing* with despair," he told *Time*'s Jay Cocks firmly, "about people trying to hold on to their dignity in the middle of a hurricane." He went on to place the album in a larger context, connecting it with his own feeling about rock, and the place of music in his life. "You've always got to remember, rock and roll's never been about giving up. For me, for a lot of kids, it was a totally positive force...not optimistic all the time, but positive. It was never—never—about surrender."

He would frequently quote from the first verse of the first tune, "Badlands," to drive home the point: "There's a statement that 'I believe in the love'...I thought that would get it, that anybody could see that."

If anybody doubted that Bruce was feeling good and strong and alive, the *Darkness* tour would soon put those ideas to rest.

PROVE IT ALL
NIGHT

*T*aking to the road with a vengeance to support *Darkness*, Bruce and the E Street Band embarked on their biggest tour yet. They averaged three-and-a-half-hour shows five nights a week for over four months during one leg of the tour. When all the totals were in, they had played to some 700,000 people on more than 120 dates in eight months' time.

If bouncing twenty-seven crew members around the country or sleeping in a tour bus as it crisscrossed the U.S. had any adverse effects on the E Street Band invasion, you couldn't tell it by the activity on or off the stage. These guys, especially Bruce, were psyched, as if the long studio period and the legal problems left behind had made every new performance that much more precious. "It's been a long and a hot summer," Bruce told New York's WNEW-FM DJ Vin Scelsa as the band entered the "home stretch" in fall of 1978.

"It's been good though. It was great to get back out.... Everybody missed it, and everybody likes being on the road for the most part."

From opening night—May 23, in Buffalo—on, the fans made it clear that they were as glad to have Bruce back as he was to see them. There was a new sound to this Springsteen tour and a new look that took into consideration Bruce's growing stature on the music scene. In acknowledging his new superstar status, Bruce made some changes in his concert appearances.

This was the first tour in which Bruce played almost exclusively in large halls and arenas, the smallest (but for a surprise one-night gig at Los Angeles's Roxy club) seating about 2,600 people. Although he was unhappy about the loss of intimacy in these huge venues, Bruce had realized that there were too many fans hoping to see him to make club dates feasible anymore. Still, he was determined to put on a show that would connect with every member of the crowd, even the ones in the long-distance seats. "The whole idea is to deliver what money can't buy," he told *Rolling Stone*'s Paul Nelson. "That's the idea of going out there. You don't go out there to deliver seven dollars and fifty cents' [then-current ticket prices] worth of music. My whole thing is to go out there and deliver what they could not possibly buy. And if you do that, you've done whatever you could do."

One of the first things Bruce did was to confront the problems of arena concert sound by devising a system that would bring out his songs with clean, crisp sound no matter what the size of the concert hall.

Working with another Bruce—Bruce Jackson, former acoustic engineer for Elvis Presley and part of the respected concert audio firm, Clair Brothers Audio— the Springsteen team came up with a concert sound system that was truly state-of-the-art. One of the most unusual things about it was the speaker system—440-pound cabinets, thirty-two of them suspended over the stage, leaving only eight between the band and the crowd. Besides providing a sound quality that few acts had been able to get at arena shows, the suspended speakers left the stage clear for Bruce's antics, which would be broadened to take advantage of the entire stage area and reach the kids in the back seats.

The two Bruces then perfected the infamous Springsteen soundcheck, a procedure that they follow to this day, and one that takes up most of the afternoon before any Springsteen concert. Running as long as four hours, each of Bruce's soundchecks is an exhausting test of the sound equipment. After a preliminary tuning, Bruce and the E Street Band take the stage and run through a number of warmup songs to get their cues straight. As often as not, the tour repertoire gives way to raucous musical jokes, novelty numbers, cover tunes, and oldies that the band never plays live. After the band is good and loose, Bruce leaves them cooking on stage to check the sound in the hall with his own ears. He takes a walking tour of the entire arena to hear the music in each section of seats, from orchestra to balcony. The mixing goes on for hours as Bruce guides the sound crew in a search for the perfect balance for all parts of the hall. It's only when the pedals on the organ are as loud and clear as the drums, Danny's glockenspiel in synch with the guitars, that Bruce will finally call the soundcheck a success.

There was another stipulation for the 1978 tour as well. Bruce requested that the first fifteen rows of every show be reserved for fans, not the press, so that he would be in direct contact with the kids who had waited

on the lines and paid their own money to come see
him.

He gave them the best rock and roll show that he
was capable of giving, night after night. While always
leaving room for an evening's particular musical whims,
Bruce concocted a basic set that showed off his band
and his new material to maximum effect. After opening
with "Summertime Blues" (or maybe "Badlands" as
autumn gained its edge on the calendar), Bruce usually
crept into the crowd with a wireless mike early on
in each show to raise "Spirit in the Night." A number of the new *Darkness* numbers appeared midway
through the first half of the show, including a fiery
"Prove It All Night" guitar duel between Bruce and
Miami Steve. From there, it was a segue from "Racing
in the Street" to "Thunder Road" and then a final visit
to "Jungleland." At this point, a good ninety minutes
into the evening, enough time and excitement having
passed from stage to audience that most rock fans would
consider it a good night's work, Bruce would announce
an intermission. This indeed was only the beginning—
there was a whole new set coming up.

And what a second half it was! "Paradise by the
Sea," a joyous trash-rocker instrumental that has never
been officially released, generally opened up the second set and pushed the pace to a high-gear rave-up
that that would only break for all to catch a breath.
"Fire," "Because the Night," and "The Fever"—all
classic tunes that Bruce gave away to other performers—were reclaimed here with blistering versions that
inevitably put their "official" releases in another category altogether. "Not Fade Away" or "Mona" (two
of Bruce's favorite covers) would bleed into "She's the
One," and "Growin' Up" frequently made an appearance with the delightful rap about talkin' to God put

in the middle break for comic relief. The anguished "Backstreets" was a show piece toward the end, and those who listened carefully would hear the origins of a new song called "Drive All Night" slowly taking shape in its central break. And then, inevitably, as the crowd was building to sheer pandemonium, Bruce would casually announce, "Wherever you are, Rosie..." and break into "Rosalita" for full-scale bedlam. "Rosalita" has become a staple of Springsteen's live shows, one of the oldest tunes that he's consistently performed and the one that you imagine will never be left out of the set. One would be hard-pressed to see "Rosalita," an exuberant cry of rock 'n' roll euphoria, performed live and not feel it was the best music being made and the most fun being had on the planet at the moment. And this was before you even got to the encore!

By the time the E Street Band finished blasting their way through "Born to Run," the Mitch Ryder medley ("Devil with the Blue Dress," "Good Golly Miss Molly," "C.C. Rider," "Jenny Take a Ride") and/or "Quarter to Three," it was obvious that Bruce's act lost nothing in its move to the big stage.

High standards and high spirits were a standard of the 1978 tour. If anyone was wondering what Bruce's family thought of their superstar son, they got a few clues during a sold-out trio of dates at Madison Square Garden, New York, in August. The first night, Bruce pulled his younger sister Pam out of the audience and dedicated Chuck Berry's "Sweet Little Sixteen" to her. He pulled her up onstage the second night as well, crying with mock outrage, "What are you doing here? It's past your bedtime!" While the audience wolf-whistled their approval of the pretty teenager and she herself blushed, Bruce beamed in big-brotherly approval. "Not bad for sixteen, huh?" he asked the crowd.

An even funnier family reunion came on the final night in New York, after the encore, when Mom Adele herself (visiting from California, where she and her husband, Douglas, live) made a guest appearance. After three hours of music, Bruce was telling the crowd that he was ready to end the show, but Mom dragged him back onstage, scolding her son and telling him to get back to work. "Aw, Mom," Bruce whined in his best little-boy style, "I can't do no more," and then kicked in for another scorcher.

The next month, during a set of gigs at the Capitol Theatre in New Jersey right around the time of his birthday, Bruce got a numbr of good-natured birthday surprises. "Oooh, socks and underwear," he kidded the fans who threw wrapped gifts onstage. But even The Boss was left speechless when a gang of ushers carried a huge birthday cake down the aisle and set it onstage before him. A scantily clad young woman emerged from the cake, confetti falling all around her, and presented Bruce with a bouquet of birthday roses. Not one to lose his cool as quickly as his speech, Bruce picked up the girl and headed offstage, laughing, before coming back for his final bows.

Bruce's actual birthday—and one of his few days off in the middle of a long stretch of touring—found him in an unusual setting for a rock star at rest. He had neither a blow-out party nor a peaceful day of relaxation. Instead, he gave an interview and a guided tour of his hometown to a reporter for a local New Jersey weekly paper.

Mike Greenblatt, editor of *The Aquarian* at the time, still finds it hard to believe. "Here it was, his only day off in the middle of a grueling six-month tour, and his birthday to boot, and he spends it with these two guys from *The Aquarian*—and with no publicist in tow. I don't know of any star of that stature that would have done that. They always have the security blanket of their publicist with them, or they're doing it in the comfort of a controlled environment. And here he is, he borrows a car, and he takes us all around. *Nobody* would have done that."

But Bruce did. From pinball at the Casino arcade to lunch at a local greasy spoon, a cruise through Freehold, and a battle on the bumper cars, Bruce took Greenblatt and photographer Bob Sorce around and about the setting of his earliest songs. "He had a borrowed orange '78 Camaro," Greenblatt goes on, "and he drove just like you would expect Bruce Springsteen to drive. His tapes were blasting in our ears—he played early Gary U.S. Bonds tapes, he played early Animals tapes, and then we started singing to them, driving down the road with the windows open and the wind rushing in our faces."

Greenblatt, whose six years as *Aquarian* music editor brought him in contact with a multitude of rock stars—and rock egos—remembers his day with Bruce Springsteen as being unlike any other interview he's ever done. "He was real pleasant and real easy to talk to; not the most articulate of people in his conversation, but he had a heavy duty charisma, a magnetic kind of quality. He approached me as another person and that was part of his charisma, that he was down to earth, and that it wasn't a star/reporter thing. After a while, it was just two guys talking, not affected at all."

Contrasted with his onstage musical onslaught, Bruce's offstage behavior on the 1978 tour was almost invariably low-key and down-to-earth. Even his one "outrageous" act said a lot about his unique approach to stardom. In the music business, where self-indulgence is the first commandment, Bruce Springsteen's wild night out consisted of...defacing a billboard of himself.

It was about two o'clock in the morning of July 4, 1978, when Bruce burst into one of the thirty rooms occupied by his touring cast and crew at the Los Angeles Sunset Marquis hotel and shouted "We're goin' to make the hit!"

On a previous evening, while driving down the Sunset Strip to catch a showing of "The Buddy Holly Story," Bruce had noticed that one of Hollywood's ever-present billboards was showing a photo of him to advertise *Darkness* and the upcoming L.A. Forum concerts. "They put up these big advertisements," Bruce groaned to WNEW-FM DJ Dave Herman, "and they paint your face real big and outta shape. My nose is long enough, but they made it like ten feet long!" Having decided that the forty-foot billboard was "the ugliest thing I ever saw," Bruce organized the E Street team to make a few "improvements."

That night at the Marquis, Clarence Clemons, Garry Tallent, and some of the road crew guys signed on for "Mission Improbable." Much to their surprise, the building that housed the doomed ad was wide open, and they had no trouble taking the elevator up some six or seven stories to the roof. With a companion down on the street handling the cop-watch, and twenty cans of black spray paint distributed to the assembled crew, they set to work. First, they painted "Prove It All Night" across the bottom of the billboard, covering over a portion of the photo of Bruce (from the *Darkness* cover). Then Bruce took over. "I wanted to write 'E Street,'" he confessed, "get the band's name up there, so Clarence says, 'Get on my shoulder.' So, I got on his shoulders and we're like six stories, five stories up, and I'm saying 'Clarence, are you tired yet?'" He laughs as he tells it. "'Cause I looked back and there's nothing but the pavement." Bruce had also hoped to add a mustache to his own portrait, but a false alarm from the cop-watcher sent the merry vandals scurrying away, Bruce and Clarence slipping down the outside fire escape like rock 'n' roll's own Starksy and Hutch.

Maybe it was the sold-out appearances at the L.A. Forum, or the special Roxy show—after all, Cher, Kiss Gene Simmons, Eagle Glen Frey, Jackson Browne, Karla Bonoff, Tom Waits, Linda Ronstadt, and Mom Adele Springsteen all would be in attendance—but Columbia Records never pressed charges. The 1978 Bruce Springsteen tour rock 'n' rolled its way onward, and no one, it seemed, could stop it from stealing the title of musical event of the year.

NO NUKES

$\mathcal{S}$eptember 21, 1979:

Backstage at Madison Square Garden in New York City, there's tension in the air. It's the third night of five scheduled "MUSE Concerts for a Non-Nuclear Future." The adrenaline is flowing, the music is blaring, and a sense of euphoric exhaustion abounds. But while other performers chat among themselves, talking happily about well-played sets or solemnly about the need for protection against nuclear madness, Bruce Springsteen moves anxiously. He leaves his dressing room, walks toward the big arena stage wings, then hesitates and returns to his room. He repeats the go-away, come-back motion a few times, and one can see the nonmusical activist hangers-on eye him nervously. What's up with this guy?

The answer is simple—nerves. This will be Bruce's first onstage appearance in nearly a year, and he's

playing in front of a sold-out crowd of some twenty
thousand people. Of course, there are the fans, who
made this particular MUSE show the fastest sellout in
Garden history when Bruce's name was added to the
bill, but there are others too—a mixed bag of California
pop music lovers and cause supporters—people who
couldn't care less about hearing "Thunder Road" and
are in the Garden to make a stand on a hot political
issue. Even for one who loves performing as much as
Bruce, the question remains "How did I get into this
thing?"

The answer, in large part, lies with the organization
of MUSE itself. The letters stand for Musicians United
for Safe Energy, a collective of rock performers making a stand against the proliferation of nuclear power
plants in the United States. The group began when
singer and songwriter John Hall realized that the effect
of the small, local antinuke benefits he had been involved with could be carried over to the huge scope
of arena-size music halls. Along with fellow musicians
Bonnie Raitt, Jackson Browne, and Graham Nash, Hall
organized the MUSE board, consisting of the musicians and four antinuke activists—Sam Lovejoy, Howard Kohn, Tom Campbell, and David Fenton. It was
the board's brainstorm to fill New York's Madison
Square Garden with the cream of the (largely Califor-
nian) rock music scene and put the money earned into
a fund for antinuclear activities. Learning from the
mistakes of previous rock benefits, many of which lost
their financial gains to the hidden costs and large over-
heads of mounting an arena-size rock concert, the
MUSE shows were planned from the start to minimize
the items that sap money away from the cause. All the
MUSE money spent would be painstakingly accounted
for, and the books would be open to the performers.

The entire event would be organized and presented by the musicians themselves in partnership with hard-working, low-profile activists. The "money people"—agents, managers, lawyers, and record company executives—need not apply. The musicians performed for expenses only, and the money raised—including that from sale of a concert program, live record album, and film—would be distributed through a MUSE foundation to national and local antinuke groups.

The high spirits of the event matched its professionalism. Putting ego, billing, and special handling aside, the performers agreed to take billing in alphabetical order and share the stage equipment so as to avoid lengthy roadie work between sets (overtime fees would kill profits if the show ran over four hours long on any night).

All told, it was a tidy little plan in keeping with Utopian ideals that had long been thought dead in the "me" decade. The original idea was for two shows—and an impressive lineup was settled—the Doobie Brothers, Jackson Browne, James Taylor, Bonnie Raitt, Hall, Nash, and assorted friends. Those shows sold well—even at the then high price of $18.50 a ticket—but it was a third and a fourth additional show that proved near instant sellouts. That's when Bruce Springsteen agreed to play for the cause.

As David Fenton explained, Bruce agreed to come after attending a Brown/Nash antinuke benefit held in Los Angeles in winter of 1978–79. "It was a show to raise funds to stop Diablo Canyon, which is a nuclear power plant built on an earthquake fault in California, and it was there that his interest in the no-nuke movement began when he talked with Jackson after the show."

In the interim period, a nuclear plant accident had

occurred at Three Mile Island, on the East Coast, and it drove Bruce to compose one of his most frightening songs, "Roulette." Never officially released, "Roulette" was a biting indictment of the bureaucratic power plays that leave people running scared and feeling helpless. Sung at a tempo that makes it sound as if the singer himself is being chased, Bruce lays it on the line—"Roulette, you're playin' with my life." If some people wondered at Bruce's involvement in the MUSE shows, a listen to "Roulette" would have convinced them that he felt deeply about the issue, although his concerns were more humanistic than political.

In fact, he would keep a low profile when it came to speaking out publicly on the issues. He would lend his support—and a healthy financial contribution it was, considering the tickets and albums sold due to his presence—but whereas each of the MUSE performers issued a statement on nuclear power to accompany their photos in the official MUSE program, Bruce fans made do with a full-page color photo of Bruce and Clarence and an insert B&W shot of the full band. No statement, no preaching, no pedantics. He would just play.

The nights he did, the predominantly "mellow" Southern California rockers who made up the MUSE lineup never quite knew what hit them. The long, low moan of sound that leaked backstage the nights of September 21 and 22 was confusing. Why would an audience that had paid good money for these star-studded shows boo every act that appeared on stage? The answer was simple—*BROOOOOOOOOOOOCE*. They were calling for the undisputed star of the night ("Too bad the guy's name wasn't Melvin or something," Bonnie Raitt joked), and that was Bruce. When he hit that stage the boolike sound turned to a roar that could have loosened the trivets holding the steel-framed building together. *This* was an alternative energy source.

Bruce cut his stage show down to less than half its usual length, but time was the only thing he cut back on. The ninety minutes played like a greatest-hits-live collection—"Badlands," "Prove It All Night," "Promised Land" (which he dedicated to Jackson Browne and the MUSE movement), "Born to Run," and more—mixed with a taste of songs being prepared for his next, the sixth, album. "The River," a new ballad, went out with a dedication to his sister and brother-in-law, and as Bruce swung one hand in a quick windmill motion at his side and played the harmonica to start it, you could hear that his music was taking yet another new direction. His vocal demanded that you pay attention, and then gave you chills when you did. In contrast to the stark sadness of "The River," though, "Sherry Darling" was a wild rave-up, and "Thunder Road" an audience participation celebration. Bouncing from side to side in the instrumental coda, jumping on top of Roy's piano for a boot-heel-on-key-board riff, or sliding across the stage on his knees to meet Clarence, Bruce seemed to be having the time of his life.

At least he did on the first night. The second night led right into Bruce's thirtieth birthday, and in an un-characteristic display of bad humor, Bruce threw a birthday cake presented to him by some fans back into the crowd. He also hauled his ex-girlfriend, who was taking pictures of him from the first section of on-the-floor seats, out of the audience and had her removed from the arena. Even Bruce himself seemed shocked by his response to the two incidents, and put the show back into high gear for a wild finale of "Quarter to Three," but it was the first, happier night that was released on film for the *No Nukes* movie. In that sequence, Bruce dazzled a new group of observers—the film critics—who took to his finale as if they were discovering a new acting talent. His shirt soaked with sweat as he swayed on swivel hips like young Elvis himself, Bruce grabbed the mike to scream, "That's all I can stand! I can't stand no more," and then collapsed on the floor. With Garry, Clarence, and Steve all lending a hand, Bruce came back to the microphone with the dazed look of a man possessed. According to his final shout—"I'm just a prisoner of rock 'n' roll!" —that's exactly what he was, and he led Clarence off the stage in a final triumphant musical exorcism. This variation on the great old soul revues led film critic Andrew Sarris to call Bruce's set "one of the most memorable male performances" for the year of 1980 in films.

If Hollywood was listening—and rumors were rife that Bruce was considering a film career—Springsteen himself had other matters on his mind. He was thirty now, a do-or-die year for many of his personal rock idols, and there was an unfinished album that just didn't seem to be falling together. The silver screen be damned—it was time to get back to the studio.

THE RIVER

*A*lthough the MUSE concerts were Bruce's first public appearance in nearly a year, he had not been idle in 1979. In fact, after a short break in California to unwind after the *Darkness* tour, Bruce jumped right into work on his next album. He had two songs from the tour that he felt were ready— "The Ties That Bind" and "Point Blank"—and he completed enough material in the first few months of the year to schedule band rehearsals in late March and recording time soon after.

Miami Steve was now officially installed as coproducer, along with Bruce and Jon Landau. Are three heads better than one? Steve seemed to think so when he described the trio's work to *Musician* magazine: "It helps if you're friends. There's a potential conflict there but on Bruce's records you know that he's running the show. But when I tell an engineer to do something one way and leave, and then Bruce walks up and tells him something else, chances are Bruce will let the engineer try it both ways and utilize the approach that works best."

Things were going well in that spring of 1979 until the mid-April day when Bruce had a minor accident. He was driving a three-wheeled off-the-road motorcycle around the grounds of his Jersey home when he banged it into a tree, damaging some of his leg muscles. Though not quite the medical drama that some media coverage made it out to be, Bruce's accident happened at a time when the album was hitting stride. The delay, short as it was, broke the momentum and put Bruce in a grouchy mood. His attitude didn't improve when, in late May, some studio tracks were leaked out of the Power Station and found their way to bootleg recordings. As much as Bruce's fans value the chance to hear his unreleased work, Bruce himself considers it an invasion of the privacy he values so much in his personal life. Further sessions for the album were placed under an even tighter veil of secrecy than usual.

The spring had happier moments, though, especially in the romantic arena, and Bruce would later speak of it being a time of songwriting inspiration. "I don't know what it is," he told reporter Kit Rachlis, "maybe the guys in the band are getting a little older, they've been with their girlfriends a long time, and they're thinking about marriage. I don't know, but I started writing love songs. Our sound man got married while I was working on the album and the wedding really got to me. I don't know how else to describe it. . . . I wrote a lot of songs after that."

Back in the studio, there were more than twenty songs under way, including "Roulette," "Jackson Cage," a beautiful love song called "Cindy" and two pieces left over from the *Darkness* sessions—"Sherry Darling" and "Ramrod." Columbia was delighted, hoping for a Christmas release of the new Springsteen album, tentatively titled *The Ties That Bind* and bearing ten new songs. A tour was even booked for the late fall and early winter of 1979, but it became clear as summer passed that the album and the tour were not going to work on that schedule. Bruce said yes to the MUSE concert appearances, but as for the record, he was in no hurry. As he explained to *Creem*'s Dave DiMartino: "I just have a feeling about the best I can do at a particular time, ya know? And that's what I wanted to do. And I don't come out until I feel that that's what I've done. Because there's so many records coming out, and there's so much stuff on the shelves. Why put out something that you don't feel is what it should be?"

The trick was, Bruce wasn't entirely sure what he wanted from this album. In fall of 1979, he had a selection of songs he was happy with, including "Cindy," "Be True," and "Loose Ends." Only the second would ever see release, as the flip side of the 1981 single "Fade Away." Shortly after the MUSE shows, Bruce decided that the new material wasn't right, and he scrapped the entire LP. Fans would have to make do with the first-ever officially sanctioned live Springsteen tracks— "Stay" and "Devil With a Blue Dress Medley" (his Mitch Ryder encore)—as they appeared on the *No Nukes* album. By now 1980 had arrived, but it wasn't a particularly happy new year, at least not yet. Bruce's decision to start over with the new LP was bringing the album budget way up and the band's spirits down. Some days he would have studio time booked, only to cancel it at the last minute.

It wasn't the writing that was difficult—there were

now over forty songs—or even the recording of them. As Roy Bittan remembered: "We recorded close to sixty different things, so it became a blur after a while. A lot of times we just did three takes on a song and it's gone. Then we'd do two other songs that night. Two weeks later, you don't remember what you did." It wasn't even the quality of the material that held up the album's release. There were simply too many songs covering too many moods for Bruce to see them working as a unified whole.

The answer came midsummer—make this a double album and let both types of material have their place. When *The River* finally broke loose, in October 1980, it sounded fresh and spontaneous in a way that belied its long and labored origins. Here were twenty songs on four sides that ran the gamut from taut, sparse ballads to instantly hummable frat-rock tunes reminiscent of beer-soaked dorm parties in the fifties. "When I did *The River*," Bruce told DiMartino, "I tried to accept the fact that the world is a paradox, and that's the way it is. And the only thing you can do with a paradox is live with it."

"I used to write a lot of stuff and throw it away," he said to another reporter, "or I'd do it in concert but not put it on an album because I thought, gee, they're just rocking songs you hear in a bar. But then I realized that those songs are me, too, just as much as the more conceptual ones, and it got to the point that I wanted to show that part. I've just now found the value and the realness of the material. So this album has more of an emotional range than my others, I think. But at the same time there's some continuity between the characters in *The River* and those on my other albums."

To some reviewers, the similarities were too close for comfort, and a debate sprang up almost immediately within the rock press—was Bruce simply sending out more songs about highways and cars?

Ira Robbins of *Trouser Press* thought so. "Unable or unwilling to cast off the cliches of his past records," he wrote, "*The River*'s attempt to make a statement is buried in an avalanche of repetition and evident lack of inspiration." Though he would credit Springsteen for "proving that you don't need to trade your soul for stardom (even if people try to do it for you)," Robbins concluded, "*The River* adds up to a water-treading exercise that neither upholds his standards of excellence nor explores any new avenues."

Julie Burchill, writing for Britain's *New Musical Express*, even took Bruce's fans to task, claiming that there was "no bore like a Bruce bore" and tossing aside *The River* as "great music for people who've wasted their youth to sit around drinking beer and wasting the rest of their lives too."

Creem, to top off another negative review, this one from Billy Altman, simply headlined it "Born to Stall."

Those who supported the album's range and saw new complexities in its familiar themes were quick to reply. In the *Village Voice*, Stephen Holden called *The River* "Bruce Springsteen's dictionary, encyclopedia, and bible of rock and roll," delighting in the playful references to the golden decade sounds of Chuck Berry, Little Richard, Roy Orbison, and Elvis. Holden addressed those who spoke of repetitions: "Springsteen said the same things just as eloquently before, but there wasn't much joy to offset the pain. It's *The River*'s lighter moments that give it the edge over Springsteen's earlier albums."

British weekly, *Record Mirror*, called it, "Four sides of pure magic; the current running strong and true throughout." *Time* magazine (U.S.) stated it this way:

"Four sides, 20 songs, a clarity and artistic ease and breadth of passion unequaled by any other rock record this year."

The controversy certainly didn't hurt sales. *The River* shipped platinum and debuted in the Top Ten of both *Record World* (at number 2) and *Billboard* (number 4), the two top music biz weeklies. One hundred and fifty AM radio stations started playing "Hungry Heart," and it was firmly in the Top Ten by December, insuring the album a healthy stay in the top regions of the charts. Ironically, Bruce had wanted to delete the song from the album, but Landau convinced him otherwise.

Bruce had broken through. Now, added to his long-time FM rock listenership—the so-called cult fans who bought every album and saw every show—was a new AM audience who had never really thought much about him before. Together, the two groups would make the 1980–81 Bruce Springsteen tour one of the hottest tickets on the concert circuit.

If intensity had been the catchword for the 1978 tour, drama was the key to the 1980–81 marathon. Again, the shows ran close to four hours each night, but this time Bruce added in a healthy share of low-key ballads and passionate monologues. The moodier numbers from *The River* were built into a quiet, introspective progression in the first half of the show, leaving most of the upbeat rockers for the postintermission rave-up.

Opening night, October 3, in Ann Arbor, Michigan, Bruce nearly forgot the words to "Born to Run" until the kids in the front row shouted them out. "And it all came back. It was like a gift," he said afterward. Later in the night, his old buddy Bob Seger came out to reprise "Thunder Road" as a duet, and the hits just kept on coming.

In New York City, where there had been enough ticket requests to fill Madison Square Garden sixteen times over, Bruce played despite having the flu and a sprained ankle, dousing his head in a bucket of ice water to keep his energy up. In New Jersey, he opened the new Meadowlands Arena, the Garden State's first major concert facility, with six sold-out nights. After the first he gushed, "That was the best show ever. . . . We couldn't hear each other onstage. I felt like the Beatles."

Backstage after a four-hour show in Milwaukee, Bruce told *Rolling Stone*'s Fred Schruers why he felt the crowds were so receptive: "The last tour, we played 122 shows, and the band played real hard every single night, ya know? Every single night in every single town, the band played very hard. And people, I think they just remembered. They remembered and this time everybody told their friends, 'You just gotta come down to the show.'"

To Bruce, every member of the crowd was an individual to be pleased. "Some guy bought his ticket, and there's a promise made between the musician and the audience. . . . I've got a lot of energy just naturally. But when I get onstage and I'm running on empty, I just think of the promise to the guy or girl who's down there, a promise that's made from hundreds or thousands of miles away. It's no different than if you stood with this person and shook his hand."

Some of the moments were chilling. In Philadelphia, it was reported that Bruce was on stage, singing "Point Blank," when news came over the airwaves that John Lennon had been murdered in New York City. The band was not told about the incident until they finished the show, and the next night, as one fan who was there tells it, "Everyone showed up with some doubt that

Bruce was actually going to play. All sorts of things had been cancelled during the day and you began to wonder if he was going to say that it would be inappropriate to play. In the crowd, there was a feeling that something isn't going to feel quite right here tonight. But they dimmed the house lights and Bruce came out in a single spotlight in the center of the stage and he started talking about how the first song he ever learned to play on the guitar was 'Twist and Shout.' He talked a little bit about Lennon and about how much he meant to him, and it was very moving. At this point it was still very much up in the air what was going to happen and then Bruce sort of turned his back on the crowd, and he had his head down and said, 'Some nights you just really don't feel like playing at all' and everyone thought 'Well, he's just not gonna be able to pull it off.' But then he said, 'But you gotta come out and play anyway,' and he broke into 'Twist and Shout' and the whole place went berserk. If anyone could have turned it from an evening of mourning into a celebration of John Lennon's music, Bruce did it as well as it could have been done.''

In Los Angeles, he made the first night of his four-show stand at the Memorial Sports Arena into a benefit for the Vietnam vets. In an impassioned speech that he would later and uncharacteristically let be used as a radio ad, Bruce spoke of the vets this way: "It's like when you're walking down a dark street at night, and out of the corner of your eye you see somebody getting hurt in a dark alley, but you keep walking on because you think it don't have nothing to do with you and you just want to get home. Vietnam turned this whole country into that dark street, and unless we can walk down those dark alleys and look into the eyes of those men and women, we are never gonna get home."

Said drummer Max Weinberg, who watched from the side of the stage, "Man, I almost burst into tears. It was one of the most emotional, moving shows we played. You've got to picture it: Bruce gives this speech... then we go onstage and on both sides of us were platforms for the paraplegics in wheelchairs. ... It was so emotional. We played for them. We played great that night."

And then there was Europe, for the first time since the "hype"-ridden quickie tour in 1975. The new invasion had to be postponed at first, due to Bruce's physical exhaustion. A statement from the Landau offices in early 1981 explained the delay:

Bruce is simply exhausted and suffering from the assorted ailments that can crop up during a grueling tour. While his health is not in serious danger, doing his first full tour of the UK without adequate rest would run the risk of later cancellations. Bruce regrets any inconvenience to his UK fans.

Once the European tour began, however, it was clear there would be no stopping it. *The River* had gone gold or platinum in each one of the ten countries the E Streeters visited this time around, and all thirty-three dates had been sold out weeks in advance. If there was concern before the tour's arrival about the language problem, opening night in Germany put it all to rest. Jon Landau described the scene: "The promoters said afterwards it was the wildest reaction that had ever taken place in Hamburg for any artist, any time. And far from not understanding the words, when it came to 'Hungry Heart,' the crowd was singing right along, half in English, half in German. Bruce was ecstatic." France, Belgium, Spain, Norway, Sweden, Switzerland, Belgium, Holland, Denmark, and the U.K. all raved for "Der Boss."

The British critics, so cool last time around, were now on Bruce's side. Said Paul DuNoyer in *New Musical Express*: "Springsteen, the man it's become common to call the last great rock and roll star, earned his long-anticipated London triumph with a solid three-hour show of passion, grit and dedication enough to put any other so-called heros to shame."

No wonder the celebration after the final European show, at London's Wembley arena, was such a blow-out. Among the guests at the backstage barbecue were Elvis Costello, Joe Jackson, Kim Carnes, and members of the Pretenders, Psychedelic Furs, and U2.

By the time the 1980–81 tour wrapped up, on September 14, Bruce had been on the road for eleven and a half months, played 139 shows, been seen by over a million people, and sold more than 99 per cent of all available seats. As Bruce described it, "This has been the best year of my life."

NEBRASKA

Bruce told me, "You reach a point where you say, 'There's too much between me and the audience—there's a board, there's a band, there's a manager.' You can leap that gulf completely by doing an album that's just you, a guitar, and a piano."

—*Bob Seger*, Musician *magazine (1983)*

*J*ournalist Ninette Beaver was puzzled. There was this guy on the phone line who said his name was Bruce Springsteen and that he wanted to talk about her book, *Caril*. The fifty-year-old assignment editor for Omaha's KMTV thought the man's name was familiar, and he said he was a musician, but she couldn't for the life of her remember just who he was. And why would he want to know about Caril Fugate, the girlfriend of a mass-murderer named Charlie Starkweather?

There would be a lot of people who wondered what Bruce Springsteen was up to in the winter of 1981–82. Recovering from the marathon pace of the just-finished American-European tour, Bruce was working on some new ideas for songs, and they were unlike any he had come up with before. Blame it on the bleak New Jersey climate in these cold months, or the nightly news reports of Reaganomics' harsh realities, but these songs were *sad*. They would be tricky ones to explain to the E Street Band, and difficult to capture on vinyl.

On January 3, 1982, Bruce decided it was time to make some demos of the new tunes. He asked E Street roadie Mike Batlin to act as engineer, using his new Tascam four-track tape recorder. Sitting in a straight-backed wooden chair in his bedroom, Bruce began to sing the songs. The chair creaked a little, and there were lyrics he still wanted to work on a bit more, but that was okay. He would fill the songs out in greater detail later with the band. Right now, it was more important just to get them down on tape, so he could hear how they were coming along.

First, he sketched them out—primarily with acoustic guitar and harmonica, sometimes adding a touch of muted electric guitar. Then he went back and put in a little echo or background vocals and just a touch of subdued synthesizer. The work went quickly, and with just Mike there to help in the taping process, it was a low-key, low-pressure recording session. Too bad studio work didn't have the same spontaneous feel as working on demos. The demos were done in a matter of hours.

In the next few days those tapes would come to haunt Bruce. There was something special about them, something powerful and provocative in the way that they were just *there*—simple and eloquent and pure. His voice was so expressive—relaxed and vulnerable in a way that's only possible when you perform alone or for a close associate like Mike.

In the next few weeks, as the E Street Band rehearsed and recorded the new songs, the feeling Bruce got from the cassette wouldn't die. The band was laying down fine tracks for the songs, but the cassette *still* sounded better. So Bruce tried some solo takes in the studio, just him and his guitar, hoping to recapture the special magic of the demos. He came closer, but not close enough. If only one could make a master disc out of thin cassette tape instead of having to transfer the material from high-quality studio tape. But then, maybe they could.... For months, Bruce and engineer Chuck Plotkin worked in L.A. to raise the aural quality of the Tascam demo tapes. By early August, they had succeeded in making a suitable master tape. Bruce decided to release this music as his next album, and he called it *Nebraska*, after the song based on the Charlie Starkweather killings.

To say that *Nebraska* caused a stir would be an understatement. When the first copies were sent out, people couldn't believe their ears. Bob Seger remembers *Born to Run* engineer Jimmy Iovine's reaction: "He said, 'This can't be it; it must be roughs.'" The FM radio stations that usually jumped on Springsteen records seemed confused. "There's almost nothing to compare it to," said one FM radio station program director. "Given the state of Album Oriented Radio, I have the feeling that most stations won't touch the album."

His words were prophetic. *Nebraska*'s sparse, acoustic sound found few friends in the tightly formatted world of rock radio. The AOR stations wanted high-energy buzz-tone guitar licks and rowdy, "let's party" lyrics, and here instead was a record that sounded like a strange cross between Woody Guthrie and Hank Williams. It was really quite ironic. After dodging the "new Dylan" tag throughout the early days of his career, Bruce had pulled a move as shocking as when Dylan had alienated his folkie fans with an electric guitar performance at Newport Folk Festival in 1965. But

Bruce had pulled the switch in reverse by pulling out the plug on his electric guitar. What's more, there was something about the songs and the way he sang them that reminded people of . . . well, early Dylan.

If the industry and fans were upset that Bruce hadn't given them the rock record they expected, Bruce was not going to let it bother him. "You've got to fulfill your expectations in yourself," he said. "I really don't care what anybody else thinks about what I do as long as I'm satisfied myself."

And if Columbia Records was secretly worried that *Nebraska* might stiff in the marketplace, they weren't saying anything to the public. "If it is played," said A&R representative Peter Philbin, "it will certainly stand out. And if it's not played on the radio, I think there'll be enough word of mouth that people will want to own the record. What this record will sell, I don't think the company knows, and I don't think Bruce really cares. It's just a statement he wants to make. We'll see how it does."

Nebraska was certified gold in December, a letdown perhaps from the platinum response to *The River* but a respectable showing for an album that had received little airplay or strong promotional activity. Bruce himself shied away from any interviews or explanations—let the music speak for itself, he seemed to say. For the most part, the critics listened attentively and liked what they heard.

In *Rolling Stone*, writer Steve Pond gave *Nebraska* four and a half stars (five makes a classic) and called it "an acoustic triumph, a basic folk album in which Springsteen has stripped his art down to the core."

Newsweek magazine put Bruce on the cover of their "On Campus" edition, for a story titled "Rock 'n' Real: Pop Music's Harsh New Message." Citing the intensity of "Springsteen's dark vision," critic Bill Barol wrote, "Unremittingly gloom is an effective way to reach the listener, one way or another: One might feel stifled, angry, unbearably sad, but not indifferent toward these songs. And when the emotion is stripped away, some exceptionally fine songs lie underneath."

The critics also wondered if *Nebraska* might be, in part, a way for Bruce to keep the sometimes stifling processes of the music industry at bay. Chris Bohn of England's *New Musical Express* noted that "by bravely ditching the excesses of the E Street Band for solo guitars, harmonica, and voice, he's made a valuable sideways leap, allowing him space to breathe again."

Another section of Steve Pond's review seconded that emotion, calling *Nebraska* "a tactical masterstroke, an inspired way out of the high-stakes rock-and-roll game that requires that each new record be bigger and grander than the last."

And Dave Marsh, longtime chronicler of the Springsteen story and frequent member of the Boss's entourage, placed the record in the context of Bruce's previous tour. Some of the audiences drawn to the 1980–81 concerts were less attentive than usual, caring more for Top Ten hits like "Hungry Heart" than for the sensitive ballads that Bruce interjects in his show. "I don't know if this decreasing sense of rapport frustrated Bruce; it would be amazing if it hadn't disturbed him somehow," Marsh wrote in *The Record*. "In any case, it seems certain that if he had released another hard rock record as sequel to *The River*, that newer, more casual audience might have buried any possibility of regaining the special relationship his best concerts created."

Not everyone enjoyed *Nebraska*, of course. Robert Christgau of the *Village Voice* dubbed it "risky" and "eloquent" but ultimately found it "boring." (There *is* something to be said of the LP's almost single-mindedly gloomy sound.) After writing about the struggle between hope and despair for so long, it seemed as if Bruce had finally called the game on despair's side—maybe life *was* hopeless. The British punk movement of 1977 had spent so much time and energy screaming "no future" that it had become pretty much a cartoon of real hopelessness. But five years later, on *Nebraska*, Springsteen outlined the cause for sorrow in such finely etched detail that the slogan "no future" seemed entirely appropriate.

Then again, for anyone who's ever comforted a friend in the throes of true despair, it is the *feeling* and the sympathy that count. In *Nebraska*, Bruce acknowledged that there are people for whom there is no real chance of a better future, no opportunity to "spit in the face of the badlands." But if he could not offer them hope, he could at least offer a record of their trials and tribulations, a salute, as it were, to their human struggles. *Nebraska* is not an easy record to listen to, but maybe it's not really there for the sake of pure enjoyment.

Love it or leave it, *Nebraska* was an album that demanded, and received, respect for flying in the face of rock fashion 1982. An insightful glimpse of the artist at work, it reaffirmed Bruce Springsteen's position as a bold, innovative performer.

If the response of a fellow performer could be considered the highest compliment to a work, Johnny Cash payed his to *Nebraska* by covering two of its songs. A kindred spirit to the plight of the hard-working common man, Cash put "Highway Patrolman" and "Johnny 99" on a 1983 album that took its title from the latter song. Though it wasn't the first time a country artist had borrowed a Springsteen tune (Emmylou Harris had put "The Price You Pay" on her 1981 Warner release *Cimarron*) or the last (Nitty Gritty Dirt Band took "Cadillac Ranch" for 1984's *Plain Dirt Fashion*, also on Warner Bros.), the others were done by "crossover" artists with one foot already (if tentatively) in the rock market. Johnny Cash's use of *Nebraska*'s tunes brought Bruce to a whole new audience and confirmed once more the extraordinary range of his songwriting talents.

BORN IN THE
U.S.A.

*T*he drums kick in with a mighty wallop, and you can almost feel the power surging through Max Weinberg's arms as he crashes down on his kit. Roy Bittan's there, too, with a clarion call of ringing piano chords. It's almost as if Aaron Copeland's "Fanfare for the Common Man" had been rewritten in the rock mode. When Bruce explodes into his opening line, you feel that's indeed what he's done. "Born in the U.S.A." is the title track to the seventh Bruce Springsteen album, an album that melds all his strengths into one stirring piece of muscular rock. If anyone felt in the wake of *Nebraska* that Bruce had slipped from the top of rock's hierarchy, *Born in the U.S.A.* was the reclamation of his championship title.

It was a long time coming. Many of the album's songs were written in the early months of 1984—"No

Surrender," in fact, was added after the record was
first turned in to Columbia Records in March—but
some date back as far as the preliminary sessions that
led to *Nebraska*. As 1982 had rolled to a close, Bruce
had a full album completed and was playing it for musician friends to get their reaction. Despite raves from
the likes of Bob Seger, that project was never released,
and in what has become a typical procedure for a Bruce
Springsteen album, the music world waited and waited
while he worked toward his own personal vision.

While he was holed up in the studio, writing, recording, and making his selection from over sixty possible songs, 1983 was a slow year for Bruce-watchers.
The quick of eye caught him in a cameo role as a car
wash attendant in Clarence Clemons's "A Woman's
Got the Power" video. Lucky clubgoers may have seen
him checking out people like the Blasters, U2, The
Bangles, or Prince in concert, or jamming with the
Asbury Park locals. On Independence Day, he partied
with friends on a seventy-foot fishing boat off the shore
of Asbury Park (he even bought a "boom box" on the
boardwalk so that he and his friends could sing and
dance to Beach Boys records), but when it came to
news of a new album, the Springsteen camp kept to
itself. In September, word leaked out that Bruce, Jon
Landau, Chuck Plotkin, and Toby Scott were in a New
York studio, mixing the final takes, but a group of fans
who caught Bruce on a New York street corner months
later heard differently. "Puleeeeze, don't ask me about
the album," Bruce said only half in jest, "because we're
going as fast as we can on it." He would only admit
that it was "*very* different" from the *Nebraska* LP and
featured the E Street Band back again and rocking with
full force.

As winter turned to spring, the light—perhaps one should say sound—at the end of the tunnel began to appear. "Dancing in the Dark" was the first clue, a single, released on May 10, 1984, and showing off a bright cushion of technopop synthesizer beneath a vintage, stay-hungry vocal. It was—dare it be said?—a dance-rock cut with hints of high-tech production aimed straight for the heart of mainstream radio.

With the single barreling up the charts, and Bruce fans stunned by the single's intriguing new sound, anticipation for the LP grew even stronger.

Columbia Records flew key retailers to Atlanta, Georgia, to hear an advance version of the record, and initiated what one record store exec called "the most expensive, best organized pre-release campaign I've ever seen." The tease was on, and it reached a peak when New York City was nearly smothered with posters of a blue-jeaned backside in front of an American flag. Maybe the men in Bruce's audience didn't react quite as favorably to that promotion as the women, but all were ready. The Boss was coming back.

On June 6, 1984, *Born in the U.S.A.* hit the racks, and nearly all who heard it agreed—this was an album well worth waiting for. As John Piccarella wrote in the *Village Voice*, *Born in the U.S.A.* was "designed to go mega-platinum and make a moral statement anyway."

The lyrics carry on in the Springsteen tradition— tough, hard-edged tales of disappointment, lost love, and hard labor. One might call this record Bruce's State of the Union address. Bruce acknowledges his homeland, is proud, no doubt, of his heritage, but fears for it as well. The lyrics, as one song repeats, are "down, down, down." Those *Born in the U.S.A.* are not always happy people, but they rock with a determination and

spirit that refuses to be beaten. From the time the title
track blasts this LP open (much like "Badlands" did
on *Darkness*) to the moment when "My Hometown"
winds it poignantly to a close, Bruce restyles all the
pop-rock influences he knows. He hooks the listener
to the catchy sounds, and slyly slips in his bleak narratives. Maybe you couldn't listen to *Nebraska*, the
album seems to say, but you can't resist listening to
this.

Few people could. *Born in the U.S.A.* fairly flew to
the top of the charts. It climbed from number 9 to
number 3 to number 1 in *Billboard* magazine in three
short weeks, and only a multiformat (black, dance, and
pop) Prince single ("When Doves Cry") could keep
"Dancing in the Dark" from the number-1-single spot.
A full half of the album's tracks were placed in heavy
rotation on rock stations throughout the country, and
record buyers overseas went wild. Britain, Canada,
Australia, West Germany, and Japan all gave Top Ten
honors to *Born in the U.S.A.* within the first month of
its release.

Controversy? That, too. Master of the disco dance
mix, Arthur Baker, was called in to do a twelve-inch
remix of "Dancing in the Dark." The resulting maxi-
single, with its boom box blaster lines and female chorus, had Bruce's die-hard rocker fans rushing to the
stereo to make sure they hadn't broken the bass knob.
The smooth Anglo-disco synth melody and mechanical
dancebeat had hard-core Bruce lovers yelling foul and
accusing the Boss of selling out, but the extended mix
made perfect sense. Bruce doesn't need to have the
"Solid Gold" dancers bumping to his music—he's
playing for higher stakes now. He knew he had a core
of fans who would follow him into the bleak dust-bowl

terrains of *Nebraska*; now it was time for the rest of the music scene to hear his message.

In spring of 1979, Clarence Clemons had told *Thunder Road*, a Springsteen fanzine, "Very few black people are into us because the exposure isn't in those areas. The radio is a tool, and the black stations won't play Bruce. They should, because the music does bridge like that."

A year before Eddie Van Halen had been asked to lay down his metal-minded guitar licks on Michael Jackson's "Beat It," Bruce was in the studio with Donna Summer. He gave her a high-energy track called "Protection" and played guitar behind the talented black vocalist. "Cover Me," the second single from the *Born in the U.S.A.* collection, was also initially recorded by Summer, but it was never released. With its "times are tough now, just getting tougher" lyric cry and modified reggae beat, "Cover Me" shared a spirit similar to that of "Dancing in the Dark," as well as to most of the songs on *Born in the U.S.A.* It was a style that welded harsh reality to a rejuvenating dance beat. If Bruce shared that style—and some audience response—with those in the black music scene, you couldn't call it selling out. It was part of a positive step forward toward social consciousness in the highly escapist world of the music biz.

Bruce *was* selling out, though—selling out every arena and concert hall that booked him in his nearly year-long *Born in the U.S.A.* tour. Besides the monumental Jacksons' tour, the Bruce Springsteen tour was *the* blockbuster event of the summer of 1984. David Geffen, head of the record label that bears his name, put it this way: "Everything else pales by comparison. It's Michael Jackson and Bruce Springsteen, and that's it." The fans agreed wholeheartedly. Unlike the tour by Michael Jackson and brothers, the Springsteen team limited their shows to halls seating five to twenty thousand people, although the rush for tickets was so great that even multiple dates in each city couldn't meet the demand.

Two shows at the Capitol Center (seating 19,287) in Washington, D.C., were sold out in three hours, and an added two nights went almost as quickly. In Wisconsin, 5,700 tickets were snapped up in just forty minutes, and a second date repeated the feat. Detroit saw 33,000 tickets go in two hours. Of course, New Jersey Springsteen fans beat all the records—202,000 tickets in only twenty-eight hours, selling at a speed *double* the hottest rate ever tallied by the ticket agency handling the show.

By opening night, June 29, in St. Paul, Minnesota, the attention directed toward Bruce's new stage act was equal to any musical event of recent memory. If Bruce was feeling the pressure—after all, it had been three years since the last tour, he was riding on his biggest album ever, and he had two new band members to break in—he carried on in his usual pre-concert manner.

There were the standard contractual requests, which were reasonable in comparison to other rockers' demands:

• Four station wagons (no limos needed, thank you) to carry the entourage to and from the hotel
• Security guards dressed in street clothes and unarmed
• A pair of first-row center seats reserved for his old friend and longest fan, Obie Dziedzic. If Obie was not in town to claim her tickets, they would go to the two fans in the seats farthest from the stage

• And, of course, enough time at each venue for the infamous Springsteen soundcheck, which had grown no less rigorous since the 1978 and 1980 tours.

"He's been running up and down the aisles, and I mean every aisle," said one astonished St. Paul security man who witnessed the soundcheck. "He's so straightforward and wonderful," added a promoter who was handling shows for the Toronto region. "It's like, 'Hi. We're doing a rock show. Make sandwiches.'"

Actually, vegetable soup is more like it. Bruce generally eats light—maybe some soup—before the show and has a big post-concert dinner long after the applause has died down. Though his taste in food still ran toward the pizza/burger/fast and ethnic end of the culinary arts, Bruce was looking better than ever on this tour. Beyond his normal "no drinks, no smokes" regimen, he was into serious body building. A two-year program of running and weight lifting gave him the physique of a Nautilus athlete, and his fancy footwork on stage gave added credence to rumors that he'd been seen around town with Michael Jackson. He looked sensational. In short, Bruce was up for this tour.

Needless to say, so was the crowd. When "Thunder Road" broke the St. Paul hall, a little past eight-thirty, it was the beginning of a three-hour-plus romance. As his newest hit explained, "You can't start a fire without a spark"—and there were more flying between the stage and the seats than had ever flown out on Main Street in the old days. Bruce was back, and though some things had changed—Patti Scialfa was here to add high-end vocals to "Out on the Street" and other numbers, Nils Lofgren was stepping in to fill Miami Steve's recently vacated shoes, and the Big Man had a new Grace

Jones—style haircut—the solid rock foundation was still strong, and fairly shaking underfoot. A new Brian DePalma—directed video would bring some of that premiere show to the rest of the world ("Dancing in the Dark") but as with any Bruce Springsteen show, there would be special moments that only those in the hall would be a part of. After all the childhood struggles to be accepted, twelve years of music industry ups and downs, and seven albums, Bruce hadn't changed his basic philosophy of performing. Each night was unique. He was giving his fans something money can't buy.

"If you think this was good," an elated Max Weinberg said after the St. Paul debut, "you should come to Jersey later on this summer. You ain't seen nothing yet!"

The shows *would* get better and tighter and even more jubilant as the tour progressed. Jersey *was* a clear highlight, but don't tell that to the crowds on the West Coast, or in Japan, or Australia, or any of the other stops on the 1984–85 Springsteen tour. Each person will tell you that they saw the best show, and in a way, they'll be right.

But there was a show that stands out for reasons beyond musicianship. It was three weeks before St. Paul, away from the media, the cameras, the entire scene of star, and moneymaking, machinery.

The sign on the marquee at Asbury Park's Stone Pony announced "John Eddie and the Front Street Runners," but they were really just the opening act that night. The air-conditioning was broken, but about one thousand people willingly sat in the sweaty little club because Bruce Springsteen had come home once more.

With radio stations scrambling to grab an advance copy of *Born in the U.S.A.*, Columbia Records fighting off the requests, and ticket scalpers salivating at the thought of another Springsteen tour, Bruce and the E Street Band took to the stage of the Stone Pony for a hometown preview of all the excitement. They played seventy minutes' worth of hot rock in this surprise appearance, with songs ranging from the old favorites ("Thunder Road," "Born to Run," "Prove It All Night") to a live premiere of most of the new LP—"Glory Days," "Darlington County," "Dancing in the Dark," "Born in the U.S.A.," and, naturally, "My Hometown."

It was a chance to get in shape for the coming tour, to try some things out, and to feel the thrill of performing once again. As always, Bruce gave a no-holds-barred show, pouring the same energy and enthusiasm into a show for those thousand people as he would weeks later for twenty times the audience. The numbers don't count with Bruce. They never did and never will. It's the feelings that count—the feelings for home, for friends, and for family. Most of all, it's the feeling for rock 'n' roll and the freedom it represents. "I think I was lucky," Bruce has said, "to find something that means so much to me as young as I was. I just wish that luck on everybody." To watch Bruce Springsteen play is to share in his luck, and whatever he does in the future, that spells good fortune for all of us who listen.

ENCORE! THE E STREET SHUFFLE

"These guys are so good, they're down to intangibles."

—*Bruce Springsteen on the E Street Band, 1975*

When the E Street Band gets together, watch out! Bruce's band is more than a backup unit. In the studio or on stage, they perform with a tightness and musical skill that comes from years of accumulated skill and friendship. And offstage, Bruce has said, "You talk to these guys, you take your life in your hands!" They're a portable party of laughs, jokes, noise, and general good-natured mayhem.

Through the years, the band has undergone some personnel changes and the music has changed with it, but the spirit of the E Street Band remains true to the days when they were just a bunch of unknowns named after a city block in Asbury Park. "Ya know," Bruce told one reporter, "you can tell by lookin' at 'em that this isn't a bunch of guys with a whole lot in common. But somehow, the music cuts right through all that."

Ladies and gentlemen, the lean machine that's still considered the '57 Chevy of rock and roll: the E Street Band.

ROY BITTAN

keyboards

"The Professor," as he's known in E Street introductions, is a formally trained musician whose first ambitions were to be a doctor. He attended Brooklyn College as a pre-med student, "but around the same time I also decided I was going to play in a band a couple of nights a week and make some bucks."

With childhood accordion lessons that had been adapted for the piano, Roy found music to be a greater pleasure than medicine and switched his college major that way, thinking he'd be a music teacher. By his last semester, however, the session offers overwhelmed the schoolwork, and "I decided I didn't want to teach anymore. I wanted to *do*." He did a lot—session work for the Archies; a road tour of *Jesus Christ Superstar*; a small-label album with a Boston-based singer named Niki Aukema. During that latter job, Roy played on a double bill at New York's Max's Kansas City with a young guy named Bruce Springsteen. "I thought he was spectacular," Roy recalled. "Everything about him intrigued me."

A New Yorker by birth (Rockaway Beach, Long Island), Roy left his Boston band to return to the Big Apple and within a week of his homecoming saw the *Village Voice* ad placed by that same Bruce Springsteen. Two auditions later, Roy Bittan was an official member of the E Street Band.

Besides adding his classically influenced skills to the Springsteen sound, Roy is one of the most in-demand session players around. He helped arrange David Bowie's *Scary Monsters* LP, produced an album for Jimmie Mack and the Jumpers, and has played on numerous hit albums by Stevie Nicks, Peter Gabriel, Meat Loaf, Dire Straits, Ellen Foley, Ian Hunter, and other top rockers. Said Mark Knopfler, of Dire Straits, "He's a perfect balance between understanding music and feeling it." Fellow E Streeter Max Weinberg describes him thus: "He's a very percussive piano player. He's also the best. Period. And he knows what to order in a French restaurant." In short, Roy Bittan has class.

CLARENCE CLEMONS

saxophone

"The Big Man," "The Master of Disaster," "The Big Kahuna," or "The Master of the Universe." Whatever you call Clarence Clemons—and Bruce seems to have a million nicknames for him—the man on the saxophone is second only to "The Boss" himself in the reaction he receives on stage.

In concert, Bruce describes his first meeting with Clarence as taking place on a dark and stormy night on the boardwalk outside an Asbury Park gig. And Bruce *says* that even he was scared. "We figured that any cat at four o'clock in the morning dressed in white, walking like there's no rain with a saxophone, was not to be messed with, right?" Well, the rain *was* really coming down, but a mutual friend really introduced the guys, and Clarence agreed to sit on a few numbers with

Bruce's then-current band, which included David Sancious on keyboards.

"We looked at each other that day and we knew— right then—where it was at," Clarence said of the fateful jam. "It was like we had been playing together for years. All the things I'd been searching for, all the bands I'd played in, everything was right there—and it blew me away. We didn't get together right away, then, but we knew it would happen."

Born January 11, 1942, in Norfolk, Virginia, Clarence came from a very devout Baptist family with several generations of preachers on his mother's side, and his father a deacon in the local church. As a child, Clarence sang in the church choir, and then traveled in the Family Four (later the Family Five) singing group with his aunts and uncles. He wanted electric trains for his ninth birthday, but his dad gave him a saxophone instead. That, however, is not the end of the story....

In high school, his thoughts turned to athletics, and Clarence earned a music *and* football scholarship to Maryland State College. He even played semi-pro ball for a while, but a car accident and a fallen-through pro deal sent him back to his horn. He was gigging at night in local bands and working days as a social worker in a boys home when he and Bruce found each other. From the old days of the Bruce Springsteen Band to the present, they have rarely been apart.

When not working with the E Street crew, Clarence likes playing with his own band—Clarence Clemons and the Red Bank Rockers, who were the house band at his nightclub, Big Man's West. The club has since closed, but the Red Bank Rockers roll on, and their first columbia LP, *Rescue*, was released in 1983. Clarence has also played on albums by Ian Hunter, Janis

Ian, Joan Armatrading, and others. He also had a cameo role as a trumpet player in the film *New York, New York*.

He's happily married to the former Christina Sandgren, a native Swede whom he met on the E Street Band's 1975 visit to Stockholm. Clarence once considered running for mayor of their adopted hometown, Sea Bright, New Jersey, but then he decided, "I don't really want to be the town mayor. I want to be the town's Big Man." It doesn't look as if anybody's dared to deny him the job.

DANNY FEDERICI

keyboards

"Now you see 'im, now you don't!" Bruce once called Danny Federici the E Street Band's "Mystery Man." He added, "All you have to know about him is hidden somewhere between his accordion and his organ."

There *is* a little more to add to that. Danny, the oldest member of the E Street Band, first started taking accordion lessons when he was seven years old. His mother would drive him to the lessons, and, as he recalled it, "She used to tell me, 'If you play music, you're going to have a good life. You'll always drive fast cars and meet beautiful women.'"

It didn't happen right away, though. Danny quit lessons when he found out that you couldn't play jazz on the accordion and first got involved with rock bands at age fourteen. He left school to work with singer/songwriter Bill Chinnock's band for a while and played with Bruce in the days of Child/Steel Mill. "I really like the shore and the ocean," he said of that Asbury Park era. "In those days it really didn't take any money to live. You could always sleep at somebody's house and drive home the next day. I was a real hippie, man; I had hair halfway down to my belly."

Danny drifted to other bands when Steel Mill broke up, but Bruce called him back into the picture shortly after recording the *Greetings* album. They've been together ever since.

When not working with the E Street Band, Danny has done session work for artists like Garland Jeffries (*Escape Artist*), Graham Parker (*The Up Escalator*), and Joan Armatrading (*Me Myself I*). When with the E Street Band—and that's his favorite place to be— Danny's the type who just might break into a medley of Italian wedding songs on the accordion during a rehearsal. He may be a "Mystery Man," but he's made no secret of his talent.

NILS LOFGREN

guitar

Although Nils Lofgren is new to the E Street Band, he's actually an experienced rocker with numerous band and solo albums to his credit.

The Swedish/Italian musician was born in Chicago in 1952, and grew up in Maryland and Washington, D.C. It was in Maryland that he first saw Jimi Hendrix play, and that inspired the sixteen-year-old boy with dreams of guitar glory. A whiz kid on both piano and guitar, Nils played in a number of teen bands before hooking up with a group called Grin. While rehearsing with Grin, Nils came to the attention of Danny Whitten, who played with Neil Young's backup band, Crazy Horse. Whitten asked Nils to play on Crazy Horse's debut LP, and Young made a similar request for Nils to work on his classic *After the Gold Rush* disc. Between the two projects, Nils became a respected rock figure at the tender age of seventeen.

The session work also helped seal Grin's recording dreams. Columbia subsidiary Spindizzy/Epic (now defunct) released *Grin* in 1971 and *1 + 1* the next year, but the band never really connected with audiences outside of a small cult following, even with critics like Robert Christgau singing the group's praises. ("Nils Lofgren is everything I think a rock and roller should be," Christgau wrote in 1972, "pugnacious, explosive, cheerful, loving.") Grin was struggling to stay alive, and the title of their late 1972 release, *All Out*, seemed to describe the band's enthusiasm as well as its music.

The next year, Nils broke from Grin to join Neil Young's band, and he toured with the singer/songwriter throughout the U.S. and the U.K. in support of Young's *Tonight's the Night* LP. When he returned to Washington he revived Grin, which got a new deal with A&M Records. The year 1973 saw the release of *Gone Crazy*, which, alas, flopped like the other Grin albums, and marked the band's final days. They officially broke up in 1974, and Nils made his solo debut the next year, with *Nils Lofgren*, on A&M Records. *Cry Tough* followed in 1976 and finally put Nils on the charts at the age of twenty four. *Back It Up!!*, an "authorized bootleg" made from a 1975 radio concert, was a fairly successful double LP, and then *I Came to Dance* (1977) gave Nils a minor FM radio hit with its title track. *Nils* was his final LP for A&M Records, released in 1979, and then he switched to Backstreet Records, where *Night Fades Away* (1981) and *Wonderland* (1983) followed.

When Bruce started his search for a replacement for Miami Steve's great guitar work, Nils was a natural. After all, they had shared the stage ages ago at a Filmore West audition night, had mutual friends, and have often been compared musically (*Trouser Press* called Nils's first solo LP "in the spirit of Springsteen"). On paper, and in concert, it sounds like a perfect match.

PATTI SCIALFA

vocals

As a close friend tells it, Patti Scialfa's story is one in the fairy-tale tradition:

"One day, she had no job. She was a singer/songwriter, bringing her tapes around and trying to get people to play on them for free. The next day, she was making a lot of money in one of the biggest bands in the world, and in St. Paul, Minnesota, in front of twenty thousand people singing with Bruce Springsteen—whom she had always loved."

If that sounds like a case for a magic wand or a fairy godmother, it was actually the end result of a decade-plus period in which the thirty-one-year-old singer kept the faith and perfected her talent. In fact, Patti first auditioned for the E Street Band when she was just seventeen, but Bruce told her to stay in school and finish before taking on another job.

Patti *did* finish school, but she stayed in touch with music by singing with various bands in the New Jersey shore area. When Billy Rush, of the Asbury Jukes, was looking to put some female vocals on a demo, Patti got involved and was featured on the Jukes' 1980 Mercury Records LP, *Love Is a Sacrifice*. Her vocal work was also heard on the *Sounds of Asbury Park* LP in 1980, and she sang on early mixes of Bruce's own "Dancing in the Dark." She's toured with both the Jukes and David Sancious (original E Street pianist) and was doing regular guest vocals with Asbury Park favorites, a band called Cats on a Smooth Surface, when Bruce asked her to audition for a spot in the 1984 E Street lineup.

He invited her over to his house one night to sing an acoustic set with him and Nils Lofgren, who had already been brought into the E Street Band. After that session, Bruce asked Patti to meet the band at the soundstage near Philadelphia where they were rehearsing for the tour. After three days, he sent Patti home, and she was convinced that it was the end of her dream. But it wasn't. The very same night that Bruce sent her back to New York, the phone rang in Patti's apartment. Once again it was Bruce, asking, "How would you like to meet me in St. Paul?" She said yes without hesitation and was on the road with the band in a matter of days.

As one Springsteen camp insider relates: "She's not just on the road for these concerts. She's actually an E Streeter now.... She's like one of the guys."

A songwriter and guitarist as well as a vocalist, Patti Scialfa is the first female to tour with the E Street Band since Suki Lahav played violin on some dates in 1974. With Patti on stage, belting out classic Springsteen songs in tandem with The Boss, other women in the audience may well be inspired to their own musical dreams.

GARRY TALLENT

bass

An old friend and coworker of "Funky" (as the band refers to him) Tallent relates that "becoming famous hasn't changed Garry at all." Physically, though, the bearded, longhaired hippie type that gazes out from the back cover of *The Wild, The Innocent, and The E Street* has given way to a cool, dark, and silent-looking guy who's clean-shaven and almost always dresses in black.

Garry, it would appear, is not the type of guy you can judge on a quick first impression. Even Bruce, in recounting how he met Garry, makes that clear: "I went up to this club [the Upstage] and I started to play my first night and this guy pulls a chair out, sits it right in the middle of the dance floor, sits down on it, and started giving me what I perceived to be dirty looks. That was Garry. I didn't talk to him for quite a while after that. I assumed for one reason or another we weren't gonna get along."

Of course, they did eventually get together, as musicians and as friends, but Garry had a number of other gigs before hooking up with Bruce for good. He was part of Bill Chinnock's band in the Upstage era, and worked with original E Street drummer Vini Lopez in *The Moment of Truth*.

A Jersey boy, Garry attended Neptune High School (Jack Nicholson is another famous alumnus) and used to leave his guitar next to the television set as a kid so that he could always listen to and practice the theme to "Secret Agent Man."

He's a tireless collector of oldies and a rockabilly

addict. The first thing he did when the E Street Band started making good money was to buy a genuine 1948 Rock-Ola jukebox and singles (more than three thousand) to fill it with.

On his occasional breaks from E Street duty, Garry has played on albums by Ian Hunter and Bonnie Tyler, was a major contributor to the *Sounds of Asbury Park* compilation, and earned associate producer credit on Gary U.S. Bonds's first LP, *Dedication* (where all the E Street Band made musical contributions).

MAX WEINBERG

drums

"Mighty" Max Weinberg joined the E Street Band in 1974, during the *Born to Run* sessions, but his fascination with the drums dates back to when he was just a kid watching the Elvis Presley band on Ed Sullivan. D.J. Fontana's drum rolls "rolled across the airwaves, filled up my senses and swept me away," as he put it, and he's gone for the beat ever since.

From second grade on, Max played and studied the drums, and was in his first band before he even hit his teens. One Weinberg group, called The Epsilons, played at the New Jersey Pavilion (Max was born in Newark) at the 1964 World's Fair; another, whose name changed from The Ides of Love to Blackstone, recorded an album for Epic Records in the early '70's. "I've done every kind of gig imaginable," Max said once. When he first auditioned for Bruce, he was, at the time, a pit musician for the Broadway musical *Godspell*. "Those were hectic times for me," Max remembered for *Thunder Road* magazine, "I was going to college during the day, playing the Broadway show at night, and then driving to a club in Jersey, do that till three in the morning, go to bed, and then do it all over."

Things got only slightly less hectic when Bruce hired Max for the E Street Band. Within ten days of his successful audition, he was on the road, leaving college and Broadway behind to live in a GMC trailer, eat the Big Man's flapjack breakfasts and work out the material that would become famous on *Born to Run*.

The proud owner of one of Ringo Starr's bass drum heads from the Beatles' 1964 tour of America, Max has never stopped being a fan or a student of his instrument. In 1984, his first book (written in collaboration with Robert Santelli) was published. Titled *The Big Beat: Conversations with Rock's Great Drummers* (Contemporary Books), it's a series of chatty talks and rhythm tips from Max and a few of his favorite stickhandlers.

His other "off-hours" activities include appearances on albums by Jim Steinman, Ian Hunter, the Asbury Jukes, and others. He's also into architecture and the movies, but the E Street Band and wife Becky remain his first loves.

AND GONE, BUT NOT FORGOTTEN...

STEVE VAN ZANDT

guitars

"*Buon viaggio, mio fratello*, Little Steven." With these words (happy voyage, my brother) in the liner notes of *Born in the U.S.A.* Bruce Springsteen bids farewell to one of his oldest friends and closest musical associates. Steve Van Zandt is on his own now, leading the pack known as Little Steven and the Disciples of Soul, who have achieved their own success with two records—*Men Without Women (Under the Gun)* (released in 1982) and *Voice of America* (1984)—on the EMI-America label.

. Van Zandt, whose original "Miami" nickname developed from his patent dislike of Asbury Park winters, had always maintained interests outside the E Street Band. An original Asbury Juke before being called into Bruce's band for the *Born to Run* sessions, Steven managed and produced for the Jukes up until the release of their third Epic album, *Hearts of Stone*, and produced songs for Gary U.S. Bonds. and Ronnie Spector.

He shared producers' credit on *The River* and *Born in the U.S.A.*, but even as Bruce's right-hand man in the studio, Steve felt the tug of his personal muse. He was "moonlighting" when he produced *Men Without Women*, but when recording sessions for *Voice of America* were completed, he knew it was time to make his break. "When I made my first record," Van Zandt told *The Aquarian* in May 1984, "we were still talking about me staying in the band, but now it is obvious that there would be incredible schedule problems. Our records are coming out at the same time, and we are going to tour at the same time. So now I have officially left the band."

As frontman for a touring unit that includes former Young Rascal Dino Danelli on drums, former Plasmatic Jean Beauvoir on rhythm guitar, and Gary Tibbs (from Adam and the Ants) on bass, "Little Steven" has become a major artist in his own right, especially in Europe, but his E Street counterpart will be missed. His unique attire (ranging from modern mobster to Goodwill street pirate) was always a visual focal point of Springsteen stage shows, while his searing guitar work and band leadership made him a Keith Richards–like spiritual center for the E Street Band's particular type of rock 'n' roll. Maybe "Miami" Steve is gone, but there's always the chance that "Little Steven" will be around in Bruce Springsteen's future. "We're still the best of friends," Steve insisted when he left the band, "and I think we'll always work together in some capacity." Here's hoping.

APPENDIXES

DISCOGRAPHY

Born In the U.S.A.
(Columbia PC 38653/UK: CBS 86304 1984)

Born in the U.S.A.
Cover Me
Darlington County
Working on the Highway
Downbound Train
I'm on Fire
No Surrender
Bobby Jean
I'm Goin' Down
Glory Days
Dancing in the Dark
My Hometown

Produced by Bruce Springsteen, Jon Landau, Chuck
   Plotkin, Steve Van Zandt
Recorded by Toby Scott
Mixed by Bob Clearmountain
Recorded at the Power Station and The Hit Factory
Mixed at the Power Station

Nebraska
   (Columbia TC 38358/UK: CBS 85669 1982)

   Nebraska
   Atlantic City
   Mansion on the Hill
   Johnny 99
   Highway Patrolman
   State Trooper
   Used Cars
   Open All Night
   My Father's House
   Reason to Believe

Recorded in New Jersey by Mike Batlin on a Teac
   Tascam Series 144 4-track cassette recorder

The River
   (Columbia PC2 36854/UK: 88510 1980)

   The Ties That Bind
   Sherry Darling
   Jackson Cage
   Two Hearts
   Independence Day

Hungry Heart
Out in the Street
Crush on You
You Can Look (But You Better Not Touch)
I Wanna Marry You
The River
Point Blank
Cadillac Ranch
I'm a Rocker
Fade Away
Stolen Car
Ramrod
The Price You Pay
Drive All Night
Wreck on the Highway

Produced by Bruce Springsteen, Jon Landau, and
    Steve Van Zandt
Recorded by Neil Dorfsman
Mixed by Chuck Plotkin and Toby Scott
Recorded at the Power Station, N.Y.C.
Mixed at Clover Recording Studios, L.A.
(except: "Drive All Night" recorded by Jimmy
    Iovine, "The Ties That Bind" recorded by Bob
    Clearmountain, "Hungry Heart" mixed by Bob
    Clearmountain)

Darkness on the Edge of Town
(Columbia JC 35318/UK: CBS 86061 1978)

Badlands
Adam Raised a Cain
Something in the Night

Candy's Room
Racing in the Street
The Promised Land
Factory
Streets of Fire
Prove It All Night
Darkness on the Edge of Town

Produced by Bruce Springsteen and Jon Landau
Production Assistance: Steve Van Zandt
Recorded by Jimmy Iovine
Mixed by Charles Plotkin and Jimmy Iovine
Recorded at the Record Plant, N.Y.C.

Born to Run

(Columbia PC 33795/UK: CBS 69170 1975)

Thunder Road
Tenth Avenue Freeze-Out
Night
Backstreets
Born to Run
She's the One
Meeting Across the River
Jungleland

Produced by Bruce Springsteen, Jon Landau, and
    Mike Appel
Engineered and mixed by Jimmy Iovine
Recorded and mixed at Record Plant, N.Y.C.
(except: "Born to Run" produced by Bruce
    Springsteen and Mike Appel, recorded at 914
    Sound Studio, Blauvelt, N.Y., engineered by
    Louis Lahav)

The Wild, the Innocent and the E Street Shuffle
(Columbia RC 32432/UK: CBS 65780 1973)

The E Street Shuffle
4th of July, Asbury Park (Sandy)
Kitty's Back
Wild Billy's Circus Story
Incident on 57th Street
Rosalita (Come Out Tonight)
New York City Serenade

Produced by Mike Appel and Jim Cretecos
Recorded at 914 Sound Studios, Blauvelt, N.Y.
Engineered by Louis Lahav

Greetings from Asbury Park, N.J.
(Columbia KC 31093/UK: CBS 65480 1973)

Blinded by the Light
Growin' Up
Mary Queen of Arkansas
Does This Bus Stop at 82nd Street?
Lost in the Flood
The Angel
For You
Spirit in the Night
It's Hard to Be a Saint in the City

Produced by Mike Appel and Jim Cretecos
Recorded at 914 Sound Studios, Blauvelt, N.Y.

Engineered by Louis Lahav
Remixed by Jack Ashkinazy
Remixed at Columbia Sound Studios

Bruce Springsteen's Gold and Platinum Albums

Greetings from Asbury Park, N.J.—GOLD—
certified 11/21/78

The Wild, The Innocent and The E Street
Shuffle—GOLD—certified 5/2/77

Born to Run—GOLD—certified 10/8/75

Darkness on the Edge of Town—GOLD—
certified 6/16/78

Darkness on the Edge of Town—PLATINUM—
certified 6/27/78

The River—GOLD AND PLATINUM—certified
12/12/80

Nebraska—GOLD—certified 12/19/82

Born in the U.S.A.—GOLD AND PLATINUM—
certified 8/7/84.

Note: The Recording Industry Association of America began platinum certification in 1976. Springsteen albums released before then are not technically considered platinum even though most of them have sold more than one million units.

A GOLD album represents a minimum sale of 500,000 units with a manufacturer's dollar volume of at least $1 million. A PLATINUM album requires minimum sales of 1,000,000 units with a manufacturer's dollar volume of at least $2 million.

Singles

Blinded by the Light/The Angel (Columbia 1973)
Spirit in the Night/For You (Columbia 1973)
Born to Run/Meeting Across the River
   (Columbia 3-10209/UK CBS 3661 1975)
Tenth Avenue Freeze-Out/She's the One
   (Columbia 3-10274/UK CBS 3940 1976)
Prove It All Night/Factory
   (Columbia 3-10763/UK CBS 6424 1978)
Badlands/Streets of Fire
   (Columbia 3-10801/UK CBS 6532 1978)
Hungry Heart/Held Up Without a Gun*
   (Columbia 11-11391/UK CBS 9309 1980)
Sherry Darling/Be True*
   (UK CBS 9568 1981)
Fade Away/Be True*
   (Columbia 11-11431 1981)
The River/Independence Day
   (UK CBS A 1179 1981)
The River/Born to Run/Rosalita (12″)
   (UK CBS A 13-1179 1981)
Cadillac Ranch/Wreck on the Highway
   (UK CBS A 1557 1981)
Atlantic City/Mansion on the Hill
   (UK CBS A 2794 1982)
Open All Night/Big Payback*
   (UK CBS A 2969 1982)
Dancing in the Dark/Pink Cadillac*
   (Columbia 38-04463/UK CBS A 4436 1984)
Cover Me/Jersey Girl*
   (Columbia 38-04561 1984)

*indicates non-album tracks.

Springsteen Material Released in Other Forms
(All are on Columbia Records unless otherwise noted)

- "Dancing in the Dark" remixes—special 12″ single
  —blaster mix
  —radio version
  —dub version
- "Santa Claus Is Comin' to Town" (live version)—7″ single and album track on *In Harmony 2*
- "Stay" and "Devil with the Blue Dress Medley" (recorded live)—album tracks on *No Nukes: The MUSE Concerts for a Non-Nuclear Future* (Asylum Records)

Springsteen Performances on Other Artists' Records

GARY U.S. BONDS—*Dedication* (EMI America, 1981)
  "Jole Blon"—support vocals
  "This Little Girl"—support vocals
  guitars and background vocals throughout
CLARENCE CLEMONS AND THE RED BANK ROCKERS—*Rescue* (Columbia, 1983)
  "Savin' Up"—rhythm guitar

GRAHAM PARKER AND THE RUMOUR—*The
   Up Escalator* (Arista, 1980)
   "Endless Night"—support vocals
LOU REED—*Street Hassle* (Arista, 1978)
   "Street Hassle"—narration
DONNA SUMMER—*Donna Summer* (Geffen, 1982)
   "Protection"—guitar, featured solo

Springsteen Material Recorded by Other Artists

(But never officially released by Bruce himself)

CLARENCE CLEMONS AND THE RED BANK
ROCKERS—*Rescue* (Columbia, 1983)
   "Savin' Up"
   "Summer on Signal Hill"—flip side of "A
      Woman's Got the Power" single
DAVE EDMUNDS—*D.E. 7th* (Columbia, 1982)
   "From Small Things (Big Things One Day Come)"
ROBERT GORDON—*Fresh Fish Special* (Private
   Stock, 1978)
   "Fire"
GREG KIHN BAND—*With the Naked Eye*
   (Beserkley, 1979)
   "Rendezvous"
DONNA SUMMER—*Donna Summer* (Geffen, 1982)
   "Protection"
POINTER SISTERS—*Energy* (Planet, 1978)
   "Fire"
PATTI SMITH GROUP—*Easter* (Arista, 1978)
   "Because the Night" (Patti Smith, co-writer)

WARREN ZEVON—*Bad Luck Streak in Dancing School* (Asylum, 1980)
  "Jeannie Needs a Shooter" (Warren Zevon, co-writer)

SOUTHSIDE JOHNNY AND THE ASBURY JUKES—*I Don't Want to Go Home* (Epic, 1976)
  "The Fever"
  "You Mean So Much to Me"

This Time It's For Real (Epic, 1977)
  "Little Girl So Fine" (Steve Van Zandt, co-writer)
  "Love on the Wrong Side of Town" (Steve Van Zandt, co-writer)
  "When You Dance" (Steve Van Zandt, co-writer)

Hearts of Stone (Epic, 1978)
  "Hearts of Stone"
  "Talk to Me"
  "Trapped Again" (Johnny Lyon and Steve Van Zandt, co-writers)
  Note: many of these songs are duplicated on *Havin' a Party with Southside Johnny* (Epic, 1979), a greatest hits collection, and *Live—Reach Up and Touch the Sky* (Mercury, 1981) a double album recorded in concert.

GARY U.S. BONDS—*Dedication* (EMI America, 1981)
  "This Little Girl"
  "Your Love"
  "Dedication"
  (Note: Four tracks on the album were produced and arranged by Springsteen and Miami Steve)

On The Line (EMI America, 1982)
  "Hold On (To What You Got)"
  "Out of Work"
  "Club Soul City"

"Love's on the Line"
"Rendezvous"
"Angelyne"
"All I Need"
(Note: Album produced by Springsteen and
Miami Steve)

Springsteen Parodies

"Born to Add"—Bruce Stringbean and the S
Street Band—*Born to Add* (Sesame Street)
"Meet the Flintstones"/"Take Me Out to the
Ballgame"—Bruce Springstone—*Live at
Bedrock* (Clean Cuts) 7" and EP
"My Life is Good"—Randy Newman—*Trouble in
Paradise* (Warner Bros.)
"Elmer Fudd Sings Bruce Springsteen"—Robin
Williams—*Throbbing Python of Love*
(Casablanca)
"On the Boardwalk"—Uncle Floyd—*The Uncle
Floyd Show Album* (Mercury)
"I Love Rock 'n Roll Medley" (includes "Born to
Run")—Joe Piscopo (as Frank Sinatra)—EP
(Columbia)
"Born to Run Things"—The MBA's—*Born to
Run Things*

VIDEOGRAPHY

"Dancing in the Dark" (from *Born in the U.S.A.*)
   directed by Brian De Palma

"Atlantic City" (from *Nebraska*)
   directed by Arnold Levine

"Rosalita" (live concert footage Phoenix, AZ,
   1978)
   [director unavailable]

"A Woman's Got the Power" (from Clarence
   Clemons and the Red Band Rockers's LP
   Rescue)
   directed by Martin Kahan
(Note: Bruce appears in cameo shot as car wash
   attendant)

FANZINE INFORMATION

American

THUNDER ROAD
P.O. Box 171
Bogota, NJ 07603

(Although it has ceased publication, back issues of this glossy fanzine are still available and recommended for those seeking additional background on Bruce, the E Street Band, Southside Johnny, and the Asbury Park scene)

BACKSTREETS
P.O. Box 51225
Seattle, WA 98115
(Quarterly magazine with interesting regular features: international discographies, news updates, and collectors' classifieds)

U.K.

POINT BLANK
c/o Dan French
11a Thirlmere Rd.
London SW 16

THE FEVER
c/o Percival
66 Norman Place Rd.
Keresley
Coventry, CV6 2BT

CANDY'S ROOM
c/o Gary Desmond
74 Winskill Rd.
Liverpool
L111HB

JACKSON CAGE
26 The Gastons
Lawrence, Weston
Briston
BS11 QZ

ABOUT THE AUTHOR

*B*orn and raised in New York City, Marianne Meyer first started writing about music while a student at New York University. With time out for staff positions on a television show (she won an Emmy Award for her work on the NBC series "Hot Hero Sandwich") and at *Record World* magazine, she has been a free-lancer ever since, contributing to *Interview*, *The Record*, *Goldmine*, *Trouser Press*, *Muppet Magazine*, a syndicated radio series, and other writing projects.

Happily married to a successful editor and excellent cook, she nonetheless succumbs to wild fantasies of sharing an intimate fried chicken dinner with Bruce Springsteen (if he'll recommend the place, she'll pick up the tab).

When not writing, she is greatly relieved, and watches the cats play in her Brooklyn backyard.